Praise for
Obstacles Welcome

Ralph de la Vega's remarkable life story is the American Dream. Starting with nothing, he built a better life through hard work, strong values and determination. The success he has achieved as a top executive at AT&T is testament to his perseverance and an inspiration to all. What makes Ralph's story so powerful is that he is living proof that opportunity exists all around us. And through his compelling story, Ralph shows how to turn almost any challenge into the opportunity of a lifetime. This is great insight for any professional or any young person aspiring to learn how to overcome obstacles and accept new challenges.

— **Randall Stephenson,**
Chairman & CEO, AT&T, Inc.

Ralph de la Vega has written a book that will be helpful to anyone who is new to the culture of business. He shares important insights and strategies for high school students deciding whether to stay in school, midcareer professionals facing new challenges in a changing economy, and those in between. De la Vega's leadership principles are a great example of public purpose capitalism—a profit model guided by integrity, a genuine concern for workers, and a commitment to providing a product that improves a community. By his example, de la Vega, demonstrates that diversity is one of America's great strengths and he describes ways to elicit the full benefits of a diverse workforce and leadership team. I recommend this book to those looking to improve their opportunities, as well as those providing leadership in this diverse society.

— **Ambassador Andrew Young,**
former U.S. Ambassador to the
United Nations
former Mayor of Atlanta,
former president of the National
Council of Churches

Ralph de la Vega tells an All-American story for our times. As an immigrant from Cuba, separated from his family, striving for education, seeking self-improvement, and achieving professional successes, Mr. de la Vega's life has embodied quintessential American values. He conveys the insights and wisdom that he amassed on his journey with the clarity and conviction that will guide other Americans in their quest.

— **Henry Cisneros,**
Executive Chairman, CityView
former U.S. Secretary of Housing
and Urban Development
former Mayor of San Antonio

The experiences gained from his personal life combined with his broad business background have enabled him to develop a value based management system that is very successful. It is that combination of rich personal and business experience that makes Ralph de la Vega a uniquely qualified leader.

— **Duane Ackerman,**
Chairman Emeritus, Bellsouth
Corporation

This is a truly American story based on one man's journey from post-revolution Cuba to the heights of professional success in the United States. It powerfully demonstrates how big dreams, hard work, and self-belief can create opportunities that change lives. Whether you are a corporate executive, a non-profit leader, a college student or just beginning high school, Ralph de la Vega's book is a compelling read. His personal tale is an inspiration for all of us in facing life's obstacles and serves as a role model for any young person aspiring to a better future.

— **Sean C. Rush,**
president & CEO, JA Worldwide

At age 10, Ralph de la Vega came to the U.S. alone and with little more than a determination to make every obstacle a positive challenge to be embraced. In so doing he has crafted a personal approach to success that he carefully and graphically chronicles. Applicable for all to follow, I can see adult or child, immigrant or native, male or female, student or professional drawing value and important inspiration from this work of love. His is the American dream and his storytelling brings history to life, be it

Cuba, hurricanes, the digital age or the merger of two corporate giants and leaves one feeling all is possible.

— **Frank D. Alvarez,**
president & CEO, Hispanic
Scholarship Fund

In *Obstacles Welcome,* Ralph de la Vega gives us a unique and compelling story of his personal and professional journey from young Cuban immigrant to an enormously successful human being. His journey is an inspirational story of leadership vision and the ability to achieve success in the face of enormous challenges and obstacles. Ralph urges us all to combine the human drive to achieve with clear vision and the commitment to care for our associates that is so critical to being a great leader.

— **Gerry Czarnecki,**
president, CEO & managing
partner, O2Media

Ralph's story and the resulting road map for life that has evolved from it contain a vital message to all of us. In a world where personal responsibility is rare indeed, Ralph describes a life formula that embraces taking responsibility for one's own destiny. We are honored to have Ralph's leadership in the Boy Scouts of America because his story and his success is the epitome of Scouting's message to young people about perseverance, goal setting, and leadership.

— **Robert Mazzuca,**
Chief Scout Executive,
Boy Scouts of America

Ralph de la Vega's story reminds us that we are all travelers, each of us seeking our own personal *American Dream.* His determination and passion light up these pages, revealing that the shaping of a single life is truly the building block of all that is good in our communities and our country. Ralph de la Vega accepted the responsibility to live his life to the fullest and he saw nothing but opportunity, regardless of the challenges that confronted him. This is a fundamental lesson for all travelers on the road of life.

—**Eduardo J. Padrón,**
president, Miami Dade College

This book is a must-read for anyone not afraid to make your dreams come true, regardless of where you are in your professional or personal life. Ralph de la Vega's life story is of a ten-year-old Cuban immigrant who came to America, penniless and without his family, and from this humble beginning, began his American journey to eventually become the current president of AT&T Mobility. Ralph not only shares his life story, but he carefully illustrates his key learnings along the way. He clearly demonstrates that with positive thinking, obstacles are really opportunities to enable one to grow beyond the expected.

— **Ernest Bromley,**
Chairman and CEO Bromley
Communications, LLC

Obstacles Welcome is the next best thing to spending hours in conversation with Ralph de la Vega. Through his conversational style, Ralph's wisdom, experience, and transparency come through wonderfully. Ralph always holds himself to a very high expectation level, serving as a uniquely special mentor and role model to folks of all ages. Young people forming their dreams and more seasoned professionals facing risk and striving for self-improvement will both welcome and relate to Ralph's very real experiences. I have had the joy and privilege of working with and learning from Ralph de la Vega. With his new book, you will too.

— **Donna Stone Buchanan,**
Chief Operating Officer, United
Way of Metropolitan Atlanta
former president, Junior
Achievement of Georgia

Without a doubt, this is one of the most inspiring books and one of the best business publications that I've read in my 40-plus years in the communications business. Ralph demonstrates true leadership principles by sharing stories and insights from his own career. His story is not only inspirational but also illustrates business values that any entrepreneur can directly apply. This book is a must-read for any young entrepreneur just starting out and a valuable resource to all professionals seeking to improve their business skills.

— **John Graham,**
Chairman, Fleishman-Hillard Inc.

Obstacles Welcome

How to Turn Adversity into Advantage
in Business and in Life

Ralph de la Vega

with Paul B. Brown

THOMAS NELSON
Since 1798

NASHVILLE DALLAS MEXICO CITY RIO DE JANEIRO BEIJING

Published in Nashville, Tennessee, by Thomas Nelson. Thomas Nelson is a registered trademark of Thomas Nelson, Inc.

Thomas Nelson, Inc., titles may be purchased in bulk for educational, business, fund-raising, or sales promotional use. For information, please e-mail SpecialMarkets@ThomasNelson.com.

Library of Congress Cataloging-in-Publication Data

De la Vega, Ralph.
    Obstacles welcome : how to turn adversity into advantage in business and in life /
Ralph de la Vega with Paul B. Brown.
        p. cm.
    Includes bibliographical references.
    ISBN 978-1-59555-264-8 (hardcover)
    1. Success in business. 2. Leadership. 3. Communication. 4. De la Vega, Ralph.
5. Chief executive officers—Biography. I. Brown, Paul B. II. Title.
HF5386.D362 2009
658.4'09—dc22   2009011877

Printed in the United States of America

09 10 11 12 13 HCI 5 4 3 2 1

This book is dedicated to my wife, Maria, and my sons, David and Mark, for the incredible support, understanding, and love they have provided me along my journey.

CONTENTS

ONE

Ninety Miles to Advantage

The Journey Begins

"Only the boy can go." Those stark words, from the mouth of the Cuban official that day at the Havana Airport, changed my life forever. It was the morning of Monday, July 1, 1962, and I was only ten years old.

My family was waiting to board a flight to Miami—my dad, Rafael; my mother, Andrea; my little sister, Barbara; and me. After months on a waiting list, we had been approved to leave Cuba and go to the United States. We had said good-byes to our relatives. The time to leave was getting short. Then a man in uniform appeared and spoke to my father. I sensed there was something wrong.

He said there were irregularities with our family's departure documents, except for mine. Suddenly my parents had a wrenching decision to make. Either we all would stay in Cuba until the paperwork was untangled, or they would send me alone and would follow as soon as possible.

My aunt Mercedes was with us at the airport. She had a friend who already had gotten out of Cuba and was in Miami. A phone call reached the friend (miraculously), who agreed to meet my plane and look after me for a few days until my mother, father, and sister arrived.

For a boy my age, all of this was a little scary but also exciting. It had the feel of an adventure. Walking across the tarmac, I looked back at my parents and sister to give them one last wave. Very shortly, I believed, we would be reunited and starting a new life in America. It was my last sight of my family for four years.

A Courageous Decision

My parents' decision to put me on that plane alone was the embarkation point of the journey this book describes. All that I believe today about how to make the most out of life traces back to that event, and to the months and years that followed as I learned to cope with obstacles, and turn them into opportunity.

I came to write *Obstacles Welcome* because of how people react to my story. Through my years as an executive for BellSouth, Bell Communications Research, Cingular Wireless, and now AT&T, I have given a lot of speeches. Afterward, as I have conversation with people in the audience, I always find that what has resonated most with them is how far I have come. While they are interested in my business experience (like integrating AT&T Wireless and

Cingular following the biggest all-cash merger in U.S. history), it is the personal saga that captivates them.

In particular, they are moved by the idea of a young boy whose family was so determined to get him out of communist Cuba, that they sent him off alone, into the care of a couple whom they barely knew. People look at me and then try to envision me as the teenager who swept floors and cleaned bathrooms in order to help his family and put himself through college. They take heart that that same child, and that same teenager, has gone on to become the president and CEO of AT&T Mobility, the wireless subsidiary of AT&T, the number one telecommunications company in America.

They want to know how I did it.

That is what I am going to explain here—so that you might grow in your own life by taking some of the same steps. The same guideposts I used then and continue to use now can make self-fulfillment and high achievement possible for you as well. They provide the foundation that will allow you to reach your most ambitious goals.

A World Turned Upside Down

In the Cuba I recall before the revolution, the de la Vegas were a conventional middle-class Cuban family. My father ran a wholesale grocery business. He worked hard and was prosperous. My mother would be called, in today's America, a "stay-at-home mom" for Barbara and me. We had many aunts and uncles who spoiled us with presents.

The de la Vega family at a beach house. *In the summer we would take vacations at the beach. In this picture, my mother is holding my sister, Barbara, while I enjoy an ice cream cone and show off my physique. That's my father in the background.*

In the pivotal year of 1959, when Castro took control, I was seven years old. The changes came quickly, and they hit hard for a close-knit family that held a strong work ethic, traditional values, and religious faith. Like millions of others, from that time on, we lived in a state of constant uncertainty and anxiety.

The freedom we had known was gone, replaced by intimidation and confiscation of property. Food distribution was taken over by the government, so my father's business was gone. Every family was given a *libreta*, or ration book, for food which became increasingly scarce. At school—including former private schools now run by the government—the staff would challenge us to pray to God for ice cream or small change. When no ice cream or money materialized, we were told to pray to Fidel for the same. At that point, the miracle of ice cream or small change would appear very quickly.

(Map courtesy of Central Intelligence Agency)

My journey began during the Cuban Revolution. Fidel Castro overthrew the government of Fulgencio Batista on January 1, 1959, and installed a socialist regime, dramatically changing the political, social, and economic fabric of the country. Located ninety miles from the United States, directly south of Key West Florida, Cuba has a population of 11 million people.

Most troubling of all were the fear and distrust that pervaded everyday life. Although no one in my close family was imprisoned, thousands of our countrymen had been locked up—and it could happen to anyone at the slightest provocation, or just a suspicion. In the community, you didn't know who among your neighbors might be watching and listening on behalf of the government. Sometimes our family had extra food through my dad's old business connections—and my mother would cook it in the middle of the night when no neighbors were awake. At school, we were told to report to our teacher if we ever heard an adult, including our parents, criticize the government. The strategy was simple—undermine loyalty to anyone and anything other than Castro and the regime.

Families like mine who had a young son had an extra worry. Boys nearing draft age (fifteen) would not be allowed to leave Cuba. There were also constant rumors swirling that Cuban boys

The de la Vega family in the late 1950s. My father, Rafael; my mother, Andrea; and my sister, Barbara. (In coordinated shirt, pants, and shoes, I appear to be on my best behavior.)

were going to be sent off to Moscow to be educated. More than any other danger, the fear of losing their children—soul as well as body—motivated families like mine to try to get out.

Applying to leave the country was a dangerous thing, however. You marked yourself as a *gusano*—a "worm." Almost immediately, militia would show up at your house and inventory all your possessions. They made it clear they would be back at the time of your departure, and every item must still be in the house. You had to leave all your possessions behind.

My wife, Maria, has even more vivid memories of these times than I do. Her family also were *gusanos*. Her father had been an accountant, and her mother had been a teacher at St. George's School in Havana. When the government took control of the school, her mother quit rather than wear fatigues and teach curriculum that was little more than propaganda. The family

My wife, Maria, with her parents, José Joaquin and Berta Martinez.

continued to attend Mass in spite of the government's open hostility to religion, and Maria remembers being in church one day when armed militia burst in, yelling and demanding that everyone get out. The priest continued with the ritual. No one moved. The militia left.

At the Halloween party at St. George's School in Havana, Maria dressed as a cat (far right). The Castro government took control of the school, forcing the faculty to wear fatigues and teach propaganda. Berta, Maria's mother, resigned her teaching position.

In January 1963, her family received a telegram that on the following day, they could sail on a Red Cross ship. Maria remembers the militia coming for the second inventory. Her mother, Berta, had a beautiful sweater, which a female militia member obviously planned to claim for herself. She told Maria's mother,

"I did not have nice things like this before Fidel." Then she told her to hand over the sweater.

Just before boarding the *Shirley Lykes* with other thankful *gusanos*, Maria's family had to pass one last checkpoint. The militia riffled through the few possessions the family was allowed to take. Maria was carrying her beloved doll, a Mariquita Pérez doll with dark hair and shining eyes like Maria's own. A guard demanded to examine it. Turning the doll over in his hands, he told his companion that the head should be torn off to make sure nothing valuable was stashed inside. Maria began to cry. The guard looked down at her and returned her doll undamaged—a rare humane act in the tension and hostility of those times.

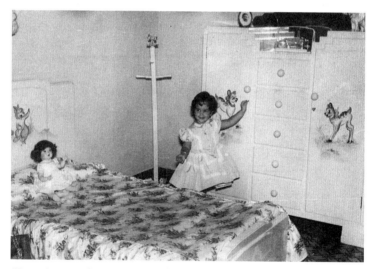

Here is Maria at home in Cuba. On the bed is her favorite doll, a Mariquita Pérez doll made in Spain. It was one of the few possessions Maria had with her when preparing to board the Shirley Lykes *in Havana Harbor. When a guard suggested tearing the doll's head off to look for contraband, Maria's tears moved him to return the doll unharmed.*

Starting Life Over

In vivid contrast, in 1962 the fledgling Cuban community of South Florida was all about humanity and compassion. Ada Baez had been in Miami only since March. Her husband, Arnaldo, who had openly opposed the revolution, had been there a little longer. He had been granted asylum in the Venezuelan embassy in Havana. He escaped to Venezuela and made his way to Miami where he was able to arrange for Ada to join him.

When I got off the plane, they were waiting—a young couple in their late twenties. Ada had worked at a retail store with my aunt, and she remembered me coming by from time to time. In 1962, Ada and Arnaldo had been married five years although separated for many months after Arnaldo's escape.

When they took me in, all of us expected that my stay would last just a few days. The days became weeks. Then, in October, the Cuban Missile Crisis ended the flow of refugees. It was obvious my parents wouldn't be coming to get me anytime soon—if ever. Occasionally I could talk to them by phone, but not too often because the calls were expensive. I would write letters and stare into the mailbox every day, waiting for a reply. There was not a lot of contact between us.

I was in a strange place where I missed my family and worried if I would ever see them again. I didn't know the language. I didn't have friends to play with. And I did not even like the food. The U.S. government had a food program for Cuban refugees that consisted of blocks of cheddar cheese and containers of Spam-like meat the size of paint cans. We called this meat *carne del refugio*—which meant "meat from the refuge." This was the only official assistance that I can recall. A steady diet of cheddar cheese and government-issued meat meant you were at the bottom of the barrel.

Initially, as I dwelled on my fate, I thought God must be punishing me. I tried to think of wrong things I had done that would explain all of this. But as time passed, I figured out that these negative thoughts were not productive. It didn't help to spend every day wondering why I was in this spot, why other children got to be with their parents and I did not. I started to realize that you can only look backward so much. Making yourself a victim doesn't change anything or help anyone—least of all yourself. You need to adapt to whatever the situation is and figure out how to make it positive.

Thanks to Ada and Arnaldo, there were plenty of positives to build upon.

They lived in one side of a duplex—which was cramped quarters to begin with, and even more so after I arrived. They gave me a small room at the back of the house as my bedroom. Being new arrivals in the United States, Ada and Arnaldo were working their way up from scratch. They had little money. Yet they shared generously with me and looked out for my well-being, just like my parents would have done. Ada asked around the neighborhood and found out how to enroll me in school.

School was difficult at first because of the language. This was long before the days of "second language" programs. Luckily for me, a few Cuban kids already were there, and I could ask them in Spanish, "What did the teacher say?" And they would translate. In that way, I began to pick up bits and pieces of English.

The nice thing about being young is that you learn quickly. I just soaked it up. By the end of the first school year, I could

One of my first pictures in the United States. *Soon after I arrived in the United States, I had my picture taken at school. I remember the shirt I wore that day. It was my favorite and a prized possession at the time.*

fend for myself—and best of all, I could help the Baezes with their English.

Ada tells a story about me that I don't remember—but I'm sure it must have happened. One day, doing my homework, I asked her to bring me a glass of water. "I'm not your maid," she replied. According to her, I answered, "One day, I am going to have a lot of maids."

That still hasn't come to pass—but the incident shows that I believed what many other of my fellow Cuban exiles believed. Hard work was going to pay off. Life was going to get better.

In my mind, Ada and Arnaldo Baez will always exemplify the remarkable achievements of the whole Cuban community who came to South Florida in those years. Back in their homeland,

I was very lucky to have had a great second set of parents. Arnaldo and Ada Baez, who took me in while I waited for the rest of my family to flee Cuba, treated me as one of their own. The Baez children, Arnie and William, became like my own brothers. Pictured are Ada and Arnaldo with their son Arnie.

some had been professionals, business owners, or executives. Now they were driving taxis, washing dishes, and working in factories—like Ada and Arnaldo did—to make a living. They did it so that their children—and their children's children—could have a better life, both economically and by experiencing the opportunities that come with freedom.

Everywhere I looked in those years, I saw unselfishness and sacrifice in action. Witnessing so much sacrifice at such a young age made a profound, life-shaping impression on me.

Starting Over Again

I was fourteen when my parents and sister arrived. It was wonderful to be back together after four years—yet there was also a bittersweet aspect. Because with my newly arrived family, I went through a second round of starting over.

By now, the Baez family had advanced economically in their four years of work. Even with the birth of their first child, Arnie, they were making progress to a more comfortable life.

But the de la Vegas were at square one—and I was there too. Back to cheese and meat in paint cans. Kids who had come over when I did were starting to have stuff. I didn't have a penny. The one good thing, for which I was thankful, was that I could make the transition a little easier for my parents and sister. I knew English. I knew how to function in America.

Like Ada and Arnaldo had done, my parents got jobs in a factory. This was the first time in her life my mother had worked outside the home. Like hundreds of thousands of other Cubans, she and my dad reinvented their lives.

For me, their experiences became yet another valuable lesson. I was learning, at a much younger age than most people, the meaning of sacrifice . . . and the power of making sacrifices in the present for the sake of a better future. Through my parents' example—dating back to the decision to leave Cuba—I could see the need to *make plans* and not just drift with circumstances . . . and to *take risks* in search of *opportunity.*

These lessons became the seeds of my future—and it's amazing how far they have brought me. The young immigrant boy without a cent to his name or a word of English has become the CEO of AT&T Mobility (AT&T Mobility is the wireless unit of AT&T. AT&T Mobility reported more than $49 billion in revenues and more than 77 million customers at the end of 2008), experiencing many wonderful adventures along the way. Very early I learned the connection between overcoming obstacles and surviving/thriving in new situations. You can use these same lessons in your own journey to create advantage from adversity.

Takeaway Points

Faith in a better future is a key enabler to overcoming incredible odds and seizing opportunities.

Courageous decisions and the willingness to sacrifice provide an enabling force to overcome the most difficult of obstacles.

The human spirit is incredibly resilient. You can start life over again and achieve your dreams.

TWO

Obstacles Welcome

Sometimes we look back on painful experiences and realize that while we never would have wished for them, they made it possible for us to grow. The long separation from my family was one example. Years later, I went through another sudden, life-changing event—this time with tens of thousands of other people. None of us wanted it to happen. Yet for many, including me, it became a unique time of personal testing and growth.

On August 24, 1992, Hurricane Andrew struck Florida with winds in excess of 155 miles per hour, devastating everything in its path. The storm caused over $30 billion in property damage, making it the costliest disaster in U.S. history up to that time. It left more than 250,000 people homeless and damaged or destroyed over 80,000 businesses. This was also the year I happened to be BellSouth's operations manager for North Dade County in South Florida (one of the areas hit by the hurricane), responsible for keeping the area's telecommunications up and running.

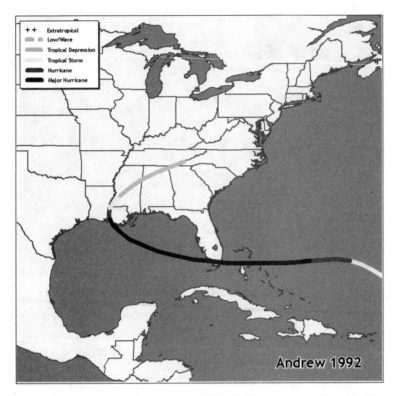

The track of Hurricane Andrew (courtesy of NOAA). The storm struck South Florida on August 24, 1992, with winds in excess of 155 miles per hour, devastating everything in its path.

In the days following Hurricane Andrew, our BellSouth team found ourselves facing destruction that is hard to describe. Entire parts of the network infrastructure were gone. We did not have power. Food and water were scarce. Traffic signals were not functioning, which made getting around South Florida a nightmare. Many street signs had blown away, so navigating the roadways was difficult. Looting became a problem, and many

(photo courtesy of AP)

The south end of South Florida was totally devastated. I had never seen damage of this nature before. Trees and power lines were down, roofs were gone, and complete subdivisions were demolished.

citizens took security matters into their own hands in order to protect their property.

In the midst of all this, our team had to find a way to restore the telecommunications infrastructure in South Florida as quickly as possible. Dealing with the aftermath of Hurricane Andrew made me all the more grateful for a truth I learned as a young immigrant and that I applied successfully in the post-Andrew chaos. I might never have discovered it if my growing up had been simpler and easier. *We must learn to overcome the obstacles life presents to us. They make us stronger, wiser, and more capable.*

That Doesn't *Seem* Difficult

Embracing obstacles sounds so simple, doesn't it? So why do we spend so much time and effort trying to avoid difficulties?

Pivotal Points—Where the Direction of Life Changes

My dramatic boyhood experience in Cuba and Miami was the first of a series of what seemed like obstacles that turned out to be great opportunities. They make up the highlights of my journey. I call them "pivotal points." What does this term mean? A pivotal point is a turbulent point in time when the decisions one makes can turn adversity into advantage, and challenges into opportunity. Throughout this book, I will refer to the pivotal points of my life as the basis of lessons I have learned—so let me acquaint you with them now.

Pivotal Point 1
The Cuban Revolution and its impact on my family

Pivotal Point 2
Guiding Bellcore TEC (Bell Communications Research Technical Education Center) through the digital communications revolution

Pivotal Point 3
Restoring South Florida's telecommunications network in the aftermath of Hurricane Andrew

Pivotal Point 4

Leading the development and deployment of Internet and Broadband Services for BellSouth

Pivotal Point 5

Turning around BellSouth Latin America during one of the worst economic depressions and some of the most unstable political situations ever in the region

Pivotal Point 6

Overseeing the merger of Cingular Wireless and AT&T Wireless, the largest all-cash merger ($41 billion) in U.S. history.

These are the pivotal points of my journey. Throughout the book, I will refer to them to explore the various lessons they taught me.

Pillars of Success

From all these pivotal points, four overarching lessons have evolved that I call "the pillars of success." They have been guideposts on my path at every turn, from Cuba to the leadership of AT&T Mobility. They can just as surely point you in the direction of success.

Here is how I visualize the pillars of success as a framework for life.

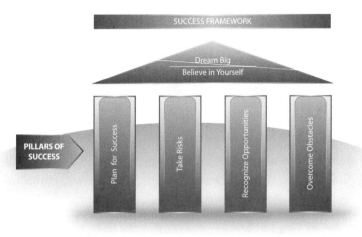

- First, hope is not a strategy. You must *plan for success.*

- Second, to get in position to achieve big goals, you must *take calculated risks.*

- Third, the big wins in life come when we *recognize opportunities.* Some people never reach their full potential because they don't see the opportunities—especially the big ones. The key is to realize that the most important opportunities are problems waiting to be solved.

And that leads to the fourth pillar, which I might never have discovered if my childhood had been less complex.

- *Embrace and overcome obstacles*—they are the best thing that can happen. They make you stronger, wiser, and more capable.

These fundamental ideas make success possible, allowing you to *dream big* and *believe in yourself.*

If you want to succeed, you need to create a plan that leads to where you aim to go. You'll need to recognize opportunities that will accelerate your journey; take calculated risks that bring you closer to the goal; and surmount the obstacles, learning from them at every step of the way.

So why don't we do this?

The answers are as varied as each of us, but there are certain commonalities. We are reluctant to take risks (or seize opportunities) because they move us outside our comfort zone . . . and/ or we are afraid of failure.

Another reason—when confronted by a roadblock, we can't figure a way around it. So we flat-out quit, settling for less than we could be. Or we try to keep from being made uncomfortable by shrinking our world and putting ourselves in situations where there won't be obstacles. The problem with either choice is that it rarely works. No matter who you are, or what you do, there are going to be obstacles that you will need to face. Some are simply inevitable:

- Unsettling change (caused by technology shifts, mergers, new projects, new bosses, transfers, a new job, etc.)
- Discouragement as a result of projects, hopes, or dreams that are thwarted
- Fear, of everything listed above, as well of the ambiguities we might encounter
- Adversity in general

How we deal with all this defines us as a person and a leader. We can either bemoan the facts, or do something about them. My belief, reinforced by the successes I have had, is that we advance by addressing and surmounting the obstacles/challenges that stand in the way . . . at work or in life. We lose ground if we shrink from them.

Your skills—especially leadership skills—will be developed through exploration, education, and self-discovery. And most of the learning occurs by facing tough times.

So I tell people—and mean it—that I feel fortunate to have experienced many difficult situations on my journey. These obstacles have put me at the right time and place to learn and grow. Confronting and overcoming your obstacles can do the same for you . . . taking you to places where you will experience the power of opportunity.

Takeaway Points

Embrace obstacles because they provide opportunities to grow in both your personal and professional life.

The Pillars of Success are a framework for achievement. You must plan for success, take risks, recognize opportunities, and overcome obstacles to reach your full potential.

Pivotal points, which are life-direction changes, provide the greatest opportunity for learning and growing. Seek them and embrace them.

THREE

Opportunities in Disguise

It was January 2000, and the Internet revolution was in full bloom. I was to lead the development of a new line of business for BellSouth: Internet and Broadband Services (see Chapter 2, my Pivotal Point 4). Some of my colleagues warned that because of the extremely ambitious goals of this initiative, it could potentially derail my career. I knew that immense challenges lay ahead—the very kind of obstacles that I had learned to welcome as opportunities in disguise.

During the 1990s several inventions and developments fueled explosive growth of the Internet. The creation of the World Wide Web and the development of Web browsers such as Netscape Navigator and Internet Explorer made the Internet user-friendly. At the same time, advances in telecommunications access technologies provided faster and faster connections to the Internet.

The Internet, combined with the telecom developments, was making lasting changes to the ways we live and work. This created unprecedented business opportunities. BellSouth put me in charge of capitalizing on them throughout its nine-state region.

At the end of 1999, just before I took the position, BellSouth had just 30,000 broadband access lines in service. My team was charged with increasing the number of broadband subscribers to 200,000 by the end of 2000 and to 600,000 by the end of 2001. This was dramatic growth by any standards, and it was far faster than the industry as a whole was expected to expand. To hit that goal, we needed to tap into the surging market by generating new users *and* taking customers away from competitors.

This required that we solve several problems simultaneously: (1) find a way to cost-effectively deploy the new technology so it would work with our existing architecture; (2) educate customers on the benefits of broadband; (3) define a way to target the right customers; and (4) build and maintain the new broadband network.

Although there were countless problems to be solved, our team didn't dwell on them as difficulties. We focused on the possibilities, and together we found ways to overcome all the obstacles.

First, we figured out how to make new and old technologies work together. This immediately turned our existing infrastructure into an enabler for broadband rather than a roadblock, as some had predicted.

Then our marketing team rolled out truly great advertising to educate customers on the benefits of digital subscriber lines (DSL), demonstrating how they provide much faster Web access without tying up your phone line, and they were always on, with no cumbersome dial-up routine.

This combination of focused, market-driven deployment with

our advertising strategy led customers to sign up in record numbers. We hit our goal of having 600,000 subscribers by the end of 2001. This made us number one in growth, number one in coverage, and number one in customer satisfaction compared with our peers in the industry.

At the end of 1999, BellSouth had approximately 30,000 broadband access lines in service. My team was charged with increasing the number of broadband subscribers to 200,000 by the end of 2000 and to 600,000 by the end of 2001. The headline above from the BellSouth Connections *publication on January 2002 says it all. Mission accomplished!*

The lessons of this assignment were multiple: To succeed with such an ambitious program, you will need: a clear vision of the future, a solid plan, an energized team, and great execution. But most important of all, we found opportunity in the problems we

faced. The result was success in the most difficult and rapidly changing of environments.

Seizing opportunities—making the most of them—is how you
change your life for the better.

As you will understand by now, "opportunity" to me usually
means a difficult situation that many people would think of as a
problem and avoid if possible. Avoidance is a mistake.

Seeing Through the Disguise

When I was asked to take the BellSouth Latin America presidency, once again there were many colleagues who advised me
against accepting the assignment because the region was mired
in many troubles. In fact, some of my best friends thought I was
crazy to consider it. As with the broadband position, I viewed the
Latin America assignment as a great opportunity.

Instead of career killers, both of these jobs proved to be just
the opposite. Were they challenging? Absolutely. But each situation gave me the chance to wrestle with circumstances I had
never confronted and learn from them. As a result, in each case
I was able to make a contribution that brought benefits to customers, increase the value of our company, and earn my spurs as
a problem-solving leader.

With broadband I was accountable for leading a line of business (LOB). Not just any LOB but one that was deemed crucial
to the future of the corporation. We were behind in Internet
services, and we needed to catch up. I had do-or-die responsibility for leading my team to overcome significant technology and

marketing challenges, and turn them into a breakthrough value proposition.

When I accepted the position of president of BellSouth Latin America in January 2002 (Pivotal Point 5), I became responsible for the wireless operations in eleven countries in Latin America (Argentina, Brazil, Chile, Colombia, Ecuador, Guatemala, Nicaragua, Panama, Peru, Venezuela, and Uruguay) which generated over $2 billion in revenues, employed fifteen thousand people, and served over eleven million customers.

I must admit, the opportunities of Latin America were very well disguised. Although the unit had grown rapidly, it wasn't profitable. Our job was to bring it into the black. That would be challenging enough, but I was given the job just in time to experience one of the most severe economic depressions and some of the most volatile political situations ever in that region.

For example, a month before I began, violent demonstrations broke out in Argentina. Clashes with police resulted in several casualties. The situation eventually led to the resignation of President Fernando de la Rua. In the next few weeks the country had a string of different presidents in quick succession. In January 2002 Eduardo Duhalde was appointed president, and our fun really began!

The Argentine peso's peg to the dollar was abandoned, and the exchange rate plunged to 4:1. Real gross domestic product fell over 10 percent. For us, this meant that overnight, revenues declined from approximately $1 billion to $250 million—pretty tough on a business plan!

Amid all this chaos, the Argentine government put enormous pressure on businesses not to raise prices to existing customers.

(Courtesy AP)

Violent demonstration in Buenos Aires, December 2001.

Obviously this put us in a bind. We were being paid in pesos worth 25 percent of their value a few moments before. But we had to buy our handsets in dollars. If we couldn't raise prices to cover the difference, this was a sure-fire recipe for bankruptcy. We had to find a way to conduct business so as to make a profit. The situation was challenging, to say the least.

We went to work.

Although we were restricted in raising prices to our base, that was not the case for new customers. So the first thing we did was to stop all promotions. We immediately increased prices for new customers who signed up. This basically brought new sales to a standstill—not a normal business goal, but better than losing money on every transaction.

With sales intentionally slowed, we had to figure out what to do with our sales force. We immediately had them turn to trying to collect past-due accounts to maximize income.

Meanwhile, a separate crisis was brewing in our largest market of the region, Venezuela. In February 2002, Venezuela let the Bolivar float freely, and the currency began to devalue at a rapid pace. Then, in April, Venezuela went through three presidents in a space of four days. Later in the year a two-month strike by businesses crippled the country. Imagine an environment where banks and shopping centers are closed, gasoline is almost non-existent, mail is not delivered, and massive demonstrations of more than one million people, both for and against the government, become commonplace.

Thriving in such turbulence was no easy task. Although most businesses closed during the strike, our industry was vital and

Demonstration in Caracas, October 2002

kept operating throughout the crisis. We had to improvise every day. A number of shopping centers where our stores were located started closing down, so we moved employees to call centers and freestanding stores. To get bills to customers, we used couriers for hand delivery!

The lack of gasoline proved a major challenge. Normally, we kept spare parts for our network infrastructure in a centralized warehouse and drove the parts to cell sites needing repairs. During the crisis we did not have enough gas to do this. So we moved the inventory to our technicians' homes, and they would bicycle the parts to where they were needed. It was as if the clock had been turned back a hundred years in operational processes, but we still had to run a modern-day cellular telecommunications business.

The huge public demonstrations were an incredible challenge. Imagine a crowd of one million, many of them with cell phones, gathering at different locations of the city at different times of the day. It was a giant floating cloud of calling activity. Our operations people worked around the clock to keep the network running.

Argentina and Venezuela were not the only crises we had to deal with in 2002. In Brazil, we were faced with the default of a billion-dollar loan when the partnership, which we will discuss shortly, did not agree to make a $375 million payment. The loan was not recoursed to BellSouth, but we still had to deal with a very volatile situation. In Colombia and Ecuador, we faced the market entry of government-backed competitors who threatened our core business.

All of this was a great learning experience. Unlike my experience at Bellcore, which we'll talk about later, this was not a situation that called immediately for a new vision. This was about bringing stability to existing operations, to give us a fighting chance for the future.

Once a degree of stability was attained, I brought our country general managers together for a planning and strategy session, a "summit meeting" of sorts. (I strongly believe in giving strategic planning responsibility to the people who will be accountable for executing the strategy.) This meeting got off to a rocky start as it became clear these GMs were used to being very independent. But we worked through it. By the end of the meeting, we had a collaborative vision, a set of strategies, and key initiatives for reaching the vision. It was hard work—but fully worth the effort. When the meeting ended, every GM literally signed the document that outlined our plan—and we went forward in unity. The net result from all this? Stellar, as shown in the chart below:

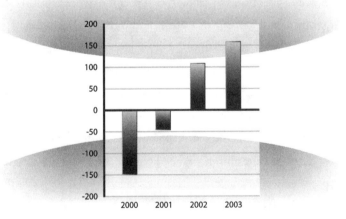

BellSouth Latin America Net Income ($M)

In Latin America, the messy batch of issues—from external politics to internal culture—seemed to doom the prospects for our business to grow in a healthy and profitable way. This opportunity turned out to be a classic example of shifting the focus away from the barriers to success, and focusing on the possibilities. When you get a group of people to zero in on what is possible instead of obsessing about what is not, they feel liberated. There is a surge of creativity, energy, and can-do spirit. (This is why market leaders should never disrespect up-and-comers.)

Ripple Effects

Seizing opportunities versus avoiding them—think of the difference this choice can make. It can cascade down through generations. For my parents and many other Cuban families, it would have been easy to avoid the danger and indignity of living as *gusanos* in a hostile atmosphere. They could have said, "It's too hard to go through this just to take a wild chance on starting over in a strange country with nothing but the clothes on our backs."

Instead, Rafael and Andrea de la Vega—and thousands like them—took the long-term view of wanting their children to grow up in freedom, able to live our beliefs, practice our values, and make the most of our abilities. They took a calculated risk in order to seize opportunity, and it has paid dividends beyond anything they could foresee.

As I take my own calculated risks, I believe that I am following in their footsteps. The decisions I've made through the years to accept challenges and confront obstacles—and the effects of these decisions on my company, my colleagues, and the communities we serve—validate the courage and foresight of my parents and all the Cuban refugees who did what they did.

Every Journey Through Adversity Needs a Compass

Putting yourself in a position to have opportunities doesn't require going through a political revolution that turns your world upside down. It *does* require that you guide yourself by the four key elements required for personal or professional achievement:

1. plan for success
2. take risks
3. recognize opportunities
4. overcome obstacles

These elements should guide you like a compass through your life.

Are You a Passenger or the Driver?

Your life is your journey—but are you driving or just along for the ride? Have you taken charge of the direction? Have you planned your destination and the route to get there? You can steer yourself toward opportunities, depending on how you plot the course.

Many people are more like passengers looking at the scenery, assuming they are stuck with whatever landscape they see out the window. I say it's *your* journey—get behind the wheel.

The Sooner, the Better

It's never too late to become the driver of your own journey and begin to turn adversity into advantage. But like many other important aspects of life, there are a lot of good reasons to get a head start at an early age.

This is a message I share with kids, especially through my involvement in Junior Achievement (JA). JA is one of my passions. More specifically, JA has been my avenue for reaching out to Hispanic students, who drop out of school at higher rates than the overall population. JA introduces them to the concepts of business and entrepreneurship, which most definitely require an education. Many Hispanic kids are being turned on to these ideas.

I tell these kids that nobody ever got ahead in business or life with the mentality of a passenger. You need to think and act like a driver—starting now. I explain that it's going to demand some sacrifice of immediate gratification for the sake of long-term advantage. It's no good to drive just a mile or two and get bored or distracted. They need to grab the wheel for the whole journey of life.

To help this point sink in for the kids, I share a story from my own days in high school. At the age of fourteen, I got a job sweeping the floor in a garment factory. It was the lowest job in the company. But I was a hard worker, which got noticed. I started to get promoted, first to cleaning and oiling the sewing machines, then to the shipping department.

Before long, I was in a sales position. This was heady stuff for a teenager, because the money seemed great. I had real responsibility, and I really liked how that felt. So I began to think this might be a pretty good future for me. Maybe I would just keep working my job, making money, and forget about trying to go to college.

At this point I always have the attention of Hispanic students in JA. Many of them are in the same situation—poor family, no money for college. The first time a decent-paying job comes along, it feels like success. It is very tempting to think, *Hey, this is good. I've got money. I can buy things and have a little fun. This is better than school.* I know how they feel—I was right there!

Unfortunately, taking this approach leads to suboptimal results. It's the opposite of taking charge of the life journey. If these kids are lucky, like I was, something happens to make this clear.

My Abuela

As I was thinking about not going to college and making the garment factory my permanent career, fate intervened. Another family member arrived from Cuba, my *abuela*—my grandmother.

Her arrival completely changed my planning. Here's how it happened.

During those years in Miami, whenever someone made it out of Cuba, all of his or her old friends would come to welcome that newcomer and celebrate. When my abuela came, it seemed that all of Miami turned out. I was amazed at the number of people who kept coming to our home. Then I figured out why.

Back in Cuba, she had been a schoolteacher. All these people coming to welcome her had been her students. She had taught them everything from Spanish and math to social studies and sciences. So

Julia Diaz Gomez, my abuela *(grandmother), was a mother of seven, a schoolteacher, and a poet. She loved to read poetry by José Martí, a poet and hero from the war of independence from Spain. Her advice to stay in school and get a degree made a huge difference in my future.*

now, her students were saying thank you. The Castro government could take their possessions, their land, their homes, but it could not take what she had given them—their education. Because of that education, they now had new jobs. New homes. New hopes. And they came in droves to express gratitude for all she had taught them.

So when she said, "Ralph, you should continue in school and get an education," it was as if all those former students were saying, "Listen to your abuela!"

Which I did. Instead of working for the immediate gain of

having money to spend, I worked to save for an education. I started planning in a long-term way—first, by taking pre-engineering courses at Miami Dade College. In these courses, I discovered I was a pretty good draftsman, so I started working part-time as a draftsman for a consulting engineering firm. Eventually, I earned enough money, with the assistance of a college loan, to obtain an associate in arts degree from Miami Dade College and then a mechanical engineering degree from Florida Atlantic University. Those degrees led to my first professional job with what was then Southern Bell. I was on my way to achieving the American dream.

I came to believe that education can unlock nearly any door. It puts you behind the wheel of your journey like nothing else can. That's what my abuela was really telling me when she said "Ralph, stay in school."

Encouragement Paves the Way

Recognizing opportunity is one thing. Having the courage to go for it is something else. You probably have noticed already that I have had a lot of help on my journey. This extends from the advice of my grandmother, to the support and sacrifices of my mom and dad, to the unselfishness of the Baez family in taking me in, to people throughout my career who have given me a chance to succeed in challenging situations.

The capstone of my four pillars of success: *Dream big . . . Believe in yourself.* That doesn't happen automatically. Encouragement from others can make a huge difference. This is why I love being involved today in Junior Achievement, and also with the Boy Scouts. These organizations excel in encouraging kids, including those who don't have many positive influences in their lives. These groups play the role that my grandmother played for me—opening the minds of young people to bigger dreams.

Now, as then, it is tough to be an immigrant kid and think of yourself as a future leader. Even after I had learned the language, at school there were cultural barriers to overcome. In my early years, I heard constant references to things like nursery rhymes and American TV shows that made no sense to me. We would start a new school year in September, and the first assignment always would be to write about our summer vacation. What would I write about? There was no money for a summer vacation for our household. Not in those years.

It's not surprising that my guidance counselors suggested I go to a vocational high school and become a mechanic. For a long time I was just an average student. I didn't see my potential any more than they did. I always felt behind and thought I would never catch up.

Then, in high school, the playing field started to level. There were new subjects like algebra and calculus, and we were all in the same boat as we learned them for the first time. I was as good as anyone, and soon I realized that I was better than most. I started getting some As. My self-confidence grew—not just because of the academics but also the promotions at the garment factory. Then my grandmother's encouragement cemented the deal. I was going to take the risk of reaching higher. I was going for an engineering degree.

Confinement in Comfort Zones

Not everyone is eager to take a calculated risk. Some people are perfectly fine staying in their comfort zone, and I don't judge that as right or wrong. Early in my telecommunications career, I was offered a major promotion to become a director at the Bell Communications Research Technical Education Center (Bellcore TEC) in Illinois. Up to this point, I had advanced rapidly through line and staff positions and had successfully completed a very tough assignment to modernize part of the BellSouth network in South Florida. This success led to the Bellcore opportunity.

This assignment became a turning point in my career. Yet it

Me with my wife, Maria, and our sons, David and Mark, at Christmas. We are seated in front of a friend's fireplace, in Naperville, Illinois.

meant moving my wife, Maria, and our young sons, David and Mark, away from our extended families in South Florida, and leaving a community that was comfortable and safe. A native-born person probably would not have even hesitated. But for us, the Cuban community of South Florida was a haven of comfort, security, familiar culture, and love.

This is one of my favorite memories from the time we spent in Chicago, seeing my boys, David and Mark, playing in the snow.

When I told my mother, she thought I was joking. Realizing I was serious, she had strong objections—"You mean to tell me you are moving your family with your two young sons to Chicago, that cold place up north?" She said this in Spanish, with Cuban vehemence that does not translate to the printed page.

Concerning relocating, I have been lucky all my adult life to have tremendous support from Maria and our sons. From a personal standpoint, it worked out well. I remember the first snow that either Maria or I had ever seen, with David and Mark making their first snow angels. We lived in a friendly, congenial neighborhood and felt at home (in every sense but climate).

The professional challenge was the pivotal point. When I arrived at Bellcore in 1985, a communications revolution was about to erupt. Digital technology was quickly supplanting analog. Data communications and fiber optics were beginning to emerge, and the entire telecommunications landscape was changing.

This was just after the breakup of the century-old Bell System, and the industry was in tremendous flux. Bellcore was jointly owned by the seven regional Bell operating companies (the largest local telecommunications companies in the country at that time). Technical excellence and training were Bellcore's primary missions. The regional Bells sent their engineers and technical specialists to Bellcore to stay abreast of "state-of-the-art" technology and operations.

At Bellcore, we had to get our people comfortable with the reality that digital technology would replace what they knew, which was analog. In hindsight, you might wonder why smart engineers would have even questioned the idea. But change is never that easy, especially change that involves the replacement of multiple billions of dollars of infrastructure and embedded technical knowledge.

To energize and galvanize them, I created a visual picture of what a digital future would like. It would be a multivendor environment with faster and much more reliable communications, capable of doing things that could hardly be imagined in 1985. As this image came to life for these engineers and technical experts, they began to accept the radical changes that we would be implementing.

This experience in developing and inspiring vision and overcoming resistance to change has proved useful to me in almost every subsequent assignment I have had since Bellcore.

I believe most readers of this book probably are aspiring to have a bigger impact in some area of their lives too. This requires shaking things up.

The best example is in making plans for a career path. You will be more valuable to your employer if you have a variety of experiences. In this age of global business, it's a fact that if you want to spend your life in one location or country, without experiencing other parts of the world, you restrict your prospects. The same is true if you stay in one type of job and don't get involved in the breadth and depth of what makes a business run.

Let me be clear: I am not judging these choices. There are valid reasons that a person might make them. But there are also a few reasons that I consider *not* so valid.

One is focusing on your limitations or on what others think are your limitations. We will talk more about this in a later chapter. But if limitations are a problem, drive your life in a direction that allows you to overcome them. This takes a plan. "If I want to reach X, I can do it in these steps."

The best opportunities usually have to be pursued, and only a driver can do that. A passenger just watches them go by. It may take a long time, but with relentless focus, you will get there.

Another invalid reason for staying inside a comfort zone relates to something we've already discussed—obstacle avoidance. Over and over in this book, we're going to see that confronting obstacles is the surest way to build momentum toward your goals.

There's one final reason for hugging your comfort zone that I consider invalid—a misunderstanding of what risk involves. Some people hear the word *risk* and equate it to jumping off a forty-story tower and having to land on a three-foot pillow. Not at all. Calculated risk is really about applying what you know and what you are good at in a new context—with the willingness to learn as you go.

There will be failures, and that is okay. The best-laid plans will sometimes go awry. It's no fun when that happens, and I remember every time I initially failed and had to regroup. Looking back, those were experiences that helped me learn to adjust on the fly.

We're going to talk more about learning from failure in a later chapter. The key is, you can never be your best without summoning up the confidence to step out and put yourself to the test.

Stay Grateful—and Laugh

Opportunity is a defining concept of the United States. It has been a powerful motivating force for more than two centuries, and it remains so today.

In this prosperous land, we get accustomed to the good life that comes from the opportunities of freedom and enterprise. We take them for granted. This can even happen to a young immigrant as he starts to climb toward the American dream. The memories of hardship recede, and the early struggles of refugee life began to dim. Then another relative arrives and reopens his eyes.

Not long after Maria and I were married, my Uncle Osvaldo came from Cuba. To celebrate, she and I took him to dinner. On the way to the restaurant, I stopped at an ATM machine to get some cash. My uncle watched with fascination as I stuck a piece of plastic into a machine, and out came money.

"I had heard these stories about America," he said, "but I never believed them. But they're true. All the money you want comes out of a machine. What a great country!" I had to explain to my uncle that before you can take money out of an ATM, you first have to earn it and put it in!

While opportunities abound, you still have to seek them and seize them to reach your full potential.

Takeaway Messages

Opportunities exist everywhere. Because they often come disguised as problems, opportunities often are not obvious. But they are always there, no matter how dire the situation initially appears. I am living proof of that.

Be your own driver—and keep your compass close! You increase your chances of discovering opportunities if you take control of your journey, making well-planned choices about where you want to go, instead of just reacting to life and the adversity that will often come.

Be comfortable with being uncomfortable. To truly have a chance to sample all the opportunities out there, be willing to venture outside your comfort zone. You may have to move or gain new skills to live the best life you possibly can.

FOUR

Learn to Unlearn and Relearn

When I first stepped into the leadership of BellSouth Latin America, the region was going through the worst economic depression in decades. Plus, we were experiencing political instability in several key countries. In addition, the business had yet to turn a profit. It was critical to reflect on what I was facing and draw from practically everything I had ever learned about what brings about success.

This led me to focus on the fact that each of the eleven countries of the region had its own political, cultural, and economic dynamics. And within the company, we had eleven different ways of doing things. In some countries we operated as subsidiaries. In others, we were in partnerships or partial ownership. In addition, in each country, the senior leadership had its own style.

Because of these differences, collectively the company had not matured from the initial developmental mode of separate markets, into an operational mode that would leverage our scale. We needed unity if we were going to win against some tough competition.

My task was to get people who were accustomed to running independent operations to work as a coordinated and cooperative team. So I put to use a past learning from my pivotal point with Bellcore. There, I had learned that in a new leadership role, there is a window of opportunity to create a vision and align people around it. This is hard to do, and it takes time. But whenever I have missed the window, I have regretted it.

In Latin America, this learning led me to call a difficult and uncomfortable—but ultimately successful—"summit meeting" of the company's top country executives to forge a united vision. It proved to be a turning point for the business.

Now, anytime I go into a new job, the first thing I do is get to know the people and involve them in building a vision for the organization.

If you just dive in, trying to solve problems without everyone having the chance to influence that greater view, then you're going to end up fighting fires all the time. People are not going to understand what you want. They are going to flounder, and eventually you will pay the price.

Learn from Your Experiences

Everyone who has worked with me knows I talk a lot about the importance of learning from your own experiences. In fact, we all go through what I call a *Learning Cycle*. It describes the process of methodically gaining knowledge, skill, and wisdom from every situation you encounter.

All of us have a wealth of experiences in career and life. Collectively, they hold more learning potential than all the books and courses that we could ever read or take. If we give those experiences the reflection they deserve, we will arrive at a set of beliefs to apply going forward. Their application leads to new experiences that will continually refresh our beliefs. As simple as it sounds, success comes from following this cycle.[1]

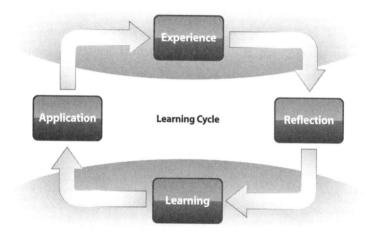

Step-by-Step

Experience

We experience new things every day. Experience comes in all shapes and sizes—as big as a challenging project at work or as small as meeting a new person and learning about his or her experiences. It's all an opportunity to learn.

The minute we stop learning and trying out new things, we start to become stagnant. We won't go much further in our growth. The pace of change around us is too fast for us to become locked in place.

With every new experience you have, make it a habit to say, "I'm going to put this in the back of my memory. The next time I run into a situation like this, I will have it as a data point of reference. I will use it."

How do we place a learning in memory? As research shows, people learn in different ways. Some are visual learners. Others learn by processing words. I think I am a little of both. As an engineer, I like to see things in schematic form—like the learning model just presented. But I also am a big note-taker. I keep a journal at work of things I have read or heard or experienced. If I see something in the *Wall Street Journal* of interest, I make a note of it right then and there. If I read a business book with an intriguing idea, I make notes as I read. Periodically, I will compile all these notes and pull them together. This serves as a refresher and allows me to draw on the learnings as needed.

Which brings us to the next step, the reflection.

Reflection

New situations can be transformed by former experiences. So the reflection stage of the Learning Cycle resembles that ancient Roman god Janus. You look backward and forward at the same time. You reflect on what you have learned from a given experience in the past, and you think about learnings from the current experience that can apply in challenges you have yet to face.

My assignment at Bellcore TEC and my Latin America experience, Pivotal Points 2 and 5, are good examples. I learned in my own career at Bellcore and BellSouth Latin America about the kind of leadership that solves problems, seizes opportunities, and avoids needless confusion. I've done plenty of reflection on those experiences, and nowadays, if you visit any organization that I lead, you will find people with a very clear vision of what needs to be done. They focus and prioritize. They don't fragment their energy on twenty things; rather, they concentrate on four or five key imperatives that need to be performed well, consistently over time. People know what they are accountable for.

Learning

Even the most unusual learning situation can have future value. You may never expect to be in similar circumstances again—then you wake up one day, and sure enough you are!

I realized this going through two of the biggest natural disasters ever to hit America—Hurricane Andrew in 1992 and Hurricane Katrina in 2005.

The biggest lesson I learned in the first of these killer storms paid huge dividends in the second. Every manager worth his or her salt realizes that employees have families and lives and concerns beyond work. Yet when an emergency threatens the business operations, sometimes the manager's first instinct is to worry about customers. What Andrew taught me is that you take care of your own people first, and they will take care of the customers. You can have the best disaster-recovery plan in the world, but it means very little if your people can't implement it because their own lives are shattered.

After living through Andrew, I never expected to apply this learning again on the same scale. Then thirteen years later came the devastation of Hurricane Katrina on the Gulf Coast.

During the record-setting hurricane seasons of 2004 and 2005, I was chief operating officer of Cingular Wireless. Drawing from the Andrew experience, we added a whole layer of preparedness to our disaster-response plan. When Katrina hit, we knew exactly where all our people were. A system was in place for getting them water, ice, and fuel. We put up our own tent city—complete with food, diapers, laundry machines, and peanut butter for the kids— for Cingular employees whose homes were damaged. We had people on hand to take care of children while their parents worked. They were assured that this little tent city would be their home as long as they needed it. The location was right next to our call center in Ocean Springs, Mississippi—so the commute was easy!

I remember a lady who worked in the call center coming up to Stan Sigman, our CEO, and myself. She asked if she could bring her grandmother to the tent city. We said, sure, of course. Right then and there, she started to cry in relief and gratitude. Her house had been blown away. She couldn't take one more thing going wrong.

Once our employees knew we were going to take care of their fundamental living needs, they were eager to refocus on work. In these situations, the impulse to help others is tremendous. Cingular's network was restored far faster than if our people had been trying to fend for themselves, bringing a big lift to the rest of the community that depended on our wireless service.

When disaster hits, put your own people first. That's the surest way to take care of your customers and get the business back up and running as fast as possible. In fact, I believe it's the only way.

Application

The application part of the Learning Cycle is where you get the big "aha!" moments.

A new experience happens. You reflect on it. You develop a set of beliefs around it, and a new theory of how things are supposed to work.

That's fine, but until you try your theory, you don't know if it holds water or leaks like a sieve. If you try it and the results are good, you have a new bit of useful, practical learning to apply going forward.

Did you ever notice how people who have been dealing with a difficult situation for a long time usually come to terms with it? They decide it can't be fixed, so it is an immutable part of reality. To get the problem solved, you have to bring new people into the mix who do not have preconceived notions of inevitability.

Observing this tendency over time, I developed the theory that putting new eyes on an old problem would lead to good results.

During my broadband days, I got the chance to test the theory in a high-stakes situation, which led to my fourth pivotal point.

With demand for access to the Internet exploding in 2000, BellSouth was accelerating deployment of technology to capture this growth. Analysts were saying that because of loop electronics in our network, our deployment was sure to experience delays and be burdened with high costs. Most of them saw this technological fact of life as a crippling negative.

It's my nature that I've never been one to accept the verdict of others that I cannot do something. So I challenged the team to take this supposed disadvantage and turn it into a competitive edge. This is exactly what happened. By modifying our remote terminals, the loop electronics were transformed into enablers instead of obstacles. We installed adjuncts with the broadband technology and connected them to existing terminals. This allowed us to repurpose our existing network infrastructure, overlaying it with broadband technology as opposed to deploying a separate network.

Nobody had used this approach before on a large scale. It was a risk, but our team was confident it could work, allowing us to reuse existing infrastructure. We deployed broadband faster and more efficiently than anyone had dreamed possible—which led to the industry-leading gains in subscribers I described earlier.

Coaches rally their team to a big upset with "bulletin board" material that appeals to their pride and unleashes their best effort. Every leadership role has taught me that when you challenge people to give you their best work, and offer them the chance to apply their talents to something meaningful, they will be inspired. You will see the impact.

Another big part of leadership is to transform work that could be drudgery into a moment in the spotlight. If you just say to an employee, "I need you to accomplish this particular task in thirty days, and give me a weekly progress report," there is no chance for heroism.

On the other hand, you can say, "I have picked you to solve a problem that looks unfixable. But I believe if anyone can fix it, you can. I don't know how you're going to do it. It's going to take some type of radically new approach, and that makes you the right person for the job." With this approach, you change the whole atmosphere. You frame the job in a way that builds confidence and makes the individual eager to reward your good opinion and trust.

Now—there is one additional point to make about the Learning Cycle.

Cleaning out the Portfolio

Every once in a while we need to clean out a lot of what we have learned, whatever the subject. It's a lot like cleaning out your closet. Styles change, your tastes change, so you get rid of some clothes that don't work anymore. The world changes too, and some of what we learned in the past doesn't apply any longer.

But many people don't sort through and discard their old, outdated ideas or ideals. Once they've built a belief set that works, they hold on to it. When a situation arises that calls for new thinking, they're locked in with the old mental framework and miss opportunities to better themselves as a person, as a business builder, or as an organizational leader.

"Keep an open mind" is easy to say, hard to do. It really means being willing to revisit, re-explore and reshape ideas we thought were permanent. Sometimes you even have to discard them altogether. Unlearning is hard work, but sometimes it is essential—as a lot of telecom engineers discovered at Bellcore in the mid-1980s when analog gave way to digital.

For many years, practically every business leader in every industry has been saying that the marketplace is changing fast—and then the next year, it changes faster still. This isn't going to stop. The need for learning and relearning accelerates too. Believing this has helped me at critical moments of my career.

Thinking Outside the Keyboard

An example of cleaning out old files is the iPhone, which AT&T Mobility helped Apple bring to market. Our company has hundreds of pages of specs for the handsets that work on our network. A good portion of them deal with the appearance and functionality of the keyboard.

Well, the iPhone doesn't have a keyboard. If you stuck with the traditional wireless industry mind-set about keyboards, you would say during the iPhone development phase, "This is a problem. A cell phone needs a keyboard." You would have started thinking of all the reasons it wouldn't work.

Or, instead of dwelling on what a phone cannot do without a keyboard, you could open your mind to an entirely new design. You could get excited about a user interface and predictive technology that eliminates the need for a physical keyboard . . . and also eliminates a lot of our detailed requirements. You could envision the millions of customers who would line up for the latest and greatest in mobile devices, a classic shift from either-or to both-and.

So this is what you can make happen when you're not locked in by past learnings and open to a better way. It's why the Learning Cycle is the key to lifelong growth and development. The conclusions in the takeaway messages may sound simple, but they have the power to change the course of your life and career.

Takeaway Messages

Every experience is an opportunity to learn and make yourself better.

Unlearning is also a part of getting better. The world is changing too fast to do anything else. Knowledge and situations change. So must we.

Be comfortable with being uncomfortable.
To truly have a chance to sample all the opportunities out there, be willing to move outside your comfort zone. You may have to move or gain new skills to live the best life you possibly can.

FIVE

Create a Compelling Vision of the Future

There is a wonderful story about three bricklayers working on the same construction project. When asked what he is doing, the first one responds, "I am making a living." The second says, "I am helping build a church." And the third says, "I am serving God."

Of the three, guess whose work was truly inspired?

Even routine work can become inspiring when it is seen as part of a big picture that adds meaning to life. What gets a group of colleagues excited? A compelling vision. A shared vision.

Even the most mundane job will become motivating if you get the people you lead (and yourself) to see it as an integral part of a compelling vision. I truly believe this, and my experience bears it out. The merger of Cingular and AT&T Wireless in 2005 shows the power of inspiring people to reach for a vision. Let me tell you what we did.

Boldness Inspires

I joined Cingular Wireless as chief operating officer in January, 2004.

Forty-seven days later, February 17 to be exact, the owners of Cingular Wireless (SBC and BellSouth) agreed to buy AT&T Wireless for $41 billion in cash (and the assumption of debt). At the time, it was the largest cash transaction in U.S. history.[1] While I was still learning my new company, Cingular, I also had to prepare to play a lead role in integrating this huge acquisition.

If any experience in my career shows that a dedicated and inspired team can make the (seemingly) impossible possible, the Cingular/AT&T Wireless merger is it.

From the time of the announcement, we knew that merging the companies was not going to be easy. The deal had to be approved by both the Federal Communications Commission and the antitrust division of the Department of Justice. Regulatory review of mergers on this scale is very intense. It goes on for months—sometimes more than a year.

In our case, speed was crucial. We needed a timetable that allowed us to get to work establishing our identity and building momentum in time for the holiday season at the end of the year. Up to 40 percent of wireless sales occur in the fourth quarter, driven by holiday shopping. The rush starts around November 15. While the same is true for many other industries, there is a special factor at work for wireless—the subscription nature of our business. If a toy maker has a down season, it's a one-time event. In wireless, the impact of signing up a new customer means monthly revenue far into the future.

Early on, Cingular CEO Stan Sigman set the goal of getting the deal approved by October 1, which would give us forty-five days to prepare a launch that had to begin on November 15, if we were to have a successful holiday season. Since AT&T Wireless and Cingular were competitors, we couldn't start collaborating until the regulators gave the go-ahead. Between the February announcement and the final approval, our ability to plan and prepare was tightly restricted. Basically the two companies had to continue operating and marketing like we always had, as all-out competitors.

Even forty-five days was going to be extremely tight, but we felt we could make it work. Why? Because we believed in our people. Given the vision of being part of an unprecedented moment in the industry, with tremendous future potential, we felt they would rise to the occasion.

Decision Time

October 1 came, and we had no approval. A week passed. Then another. And another. Finally, word came on October 26 that all the hurdles were cleared. While this was record approval time for such a large merger, we had lost nearly four precious weeks of our planned run-up to launch.

So now, the leadership team of Cingular faced the kind of decision that shapes destiny. One choice was to defer launching the combined company until the first quarter of 2005, playing it safe with a deliberate and careful integration. In this scenario, the two companies would continue to operate separately for at least a couple of months. This would allow for a methodical transition. But it also would dilute a lot of the momentum and excitement, missing the holidays entirely and significantly delaying the advantage of becoming the nation's largest wireless carrier with the most extensive network. And it would give competitors an open invitation to come after our customers while we were slowly redefining ourselves.

Or, we could make the choice to go for it. This meant launching a full, comprehensive, all-out drive toward integration—people, training, network, branding, retail makeover, everything—in time for a November 15 launch.

Could our people make this happen, now that the window of opportunity had been narrowed so dramatically? The question made me appreciate how a football coach must feel right before his team takes the field for a huge game. After eight months of initial planning and preparation, I knew we were ready.

Confidence in Our People

On October 26, within two hours of being notified of governmental approval, we closed the deal with a wire transaction of $41 billion in cash. If you were using an ATM that morning, you might have felt tremors as all that money moved through the system.

Now we had less than three weeks—456 hours, to be exact—to make the most of it. We would attempt to pull off what everyone (but a few of us) said was impossible: create in nineteen days the nation's largest wireless company by combining Cingular Wireless and AT&T Wireless.

What did we need to accomplish? For starters, two mobile networks had to be combined into one. While this process would continue for many months, basic compatibility had to be established right away, so that by November 15, AT&T Wireless users could make and receive calls on the Cingular network, and vice versa. We had to accomplish this in a way that avoided disruptions for customers. As an adjunct of combining the networks, we also had to create a unified billing system.

Another huge task was retail conversion. We had to renovate and rebrand more than eleven hundred AT&T stores with Cingular's retail format: new fixtures, new colors and logo, product literature, and, of course, new phones. Prior to approval, we had done some preparation for this, like ordering Cingular shirts for AT&T Wireless sales employees. New signage and marketing materials were ready to go. Of course, there was the possibility of eating these costs if the approval didn't come. But the time these steps would save was worth that risk.

Most challenging of all, we had to combine two workforces of about thirty thousand employees each—two different cultures, traditions, and ways of working—and do it in a manner that primed everyone to be ready to serve 46 million subscribers flawlessly on day 1.

What made us think we could make this fast-track launch work? The same confidence in our people that shaped our thinking about a forty-five-day implementation window now came to the fore in the new situation. If anyone could make it happen in nineteen days, our people could.

Flawless Execution

The two-minute drill in football depends on everybody knowing how to execute each play effectively, in the least time possible. Our launch preparation was all about having the vision, leadership, and speed and everybody having a clear picture of what to do.

Immediately we announced the top fifty-three leaders—based on management reviews that identified the best of the best in both companies. Of our four regional presidents, two came from Cingular, and two came from AT&T Wireless. When we named our network team, two of the four regional VPs came from Cingular Wireless, and two came from AT&T Wireless. This was not by manipulation or design. We did not plan on a fifty/fifty split between the companies. It was simply the way it worked out, once we committed to selecting the best people.

Our message to everyone in each company was this: We are going to take two good companies and create one great one. And we are going to do it in record time. This will be one of the most difficult things you ever will undertake. To be part of it will involve sacrifice and time away from your family. But once it is done, it is going to be something you will look back at forever and say, "I was a part of that. They couldn't have done it without me."

We put a bold vision in front of our people: to be the most

highly regarded wireless company in the world, with a driving focus around sales and service.

The goals we articulated were extremely daring. We wanted:

- to be number one in market share

- to be number one in flow share (market share growth)

- to experience industry-leading profitability

- to be the company our customers were most willing to recommend

- to be an employer of choice

The day after the deal closed, the fifty-three leaders came to Atlanta, and we shared the vision, mission, and key strategies for the new company. The next day we assembled another three hundred leaders—also carefully chosen from both companies based on the key roles they would play. In an incredibly uplifting kickoff, we shared our plans with them.

Part of the event was a powerful video by John Madden explaining what it takes to be a champion. You could feel the effect, like a team getting ready to roar out of the tunnel and settle for nothing less than the title.

Inspiration and vision are a great start for any project. The next step is to translate that into solid results. Each leader of the new Cingular Wireless returned to his or her market with a game plan and playbooks, detailing the steps and milestones of the next nineteen days. The work wasn't easy, but the playbooks made the task extremely clear. We developed them during the eight months between the merger's announcement and final approval.

We had sixty thousand playbooks, with different versions for sales, network IT, and all other functions. Everyone knew exactly what he or she should be doing in the next 456 hours.

To achieve the vision and goals of the merger, we established four strategic imperatives, our "must do's." Through these four imperatives, we brought focus and energized the new company. There was clarity and direction, rather than a vacuum. Vacuums are breeding grounds for confusion, culture wars, and turf clashes.

The four strategic imperatives that prevented a vacuum at Cingular Wireless are shown in the following graphic.

Cingular Strategic Imperatives

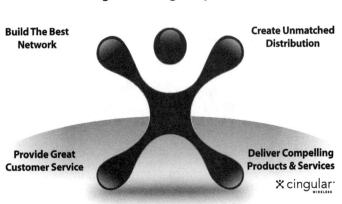

Build The Best Network

Create Unmatched Distribution

Provide Great Customer Service

Deliver Compelling Products & Services

✕ cingular·

The effort fanned out from leaders throughout the company. Imagine sixty-thousand people turning on a dime, from fierce competition to total cooperation. In total, we spent over one million hours training more than one hundred thousand people, including our agents and suppliers. At the same time, we deployed new phones and new marketing materials to prepare for remerchandising and rebranding every former AT&T Wireless store.

The makeover of the stores took place literally overnight— Sunday, November 14, between 6 p.m. and midnight. Right on time Monday morning, all eleven hundred stores were open for business under the Cingular name, signage, and colors, with Cingular products and material.

Celebrating the completion of the rebranding to Cingular Wireless. This picture was taken on November 14, 2004, around midnight. It was the final step in completing the merger-integration plans before launching the new company ahead of the holiday season on November 15, 2004.

Expectations Exceeded

This entire effort was an incredible feat by a group of people most of whom had not a chance to work together or even meet prior to the merger. It confirmed a conviction I had based my entire career on: if you give people an inspiring vision and clear direction about their role, the sky is the limit.

It was remarkable how well things went from the start—just like we had hoped for months before when the merger was first conceived. To an amazing extent, we looked and acted like a smooth-running machine from the first hour of business. Our new color scheme of blue and orange combined the visual palette of the former companies. We had a compelling new tagline: Raising the Bar. We also had an exciting new product to introduce: the Motorola RAZR, an iconic handset exclusive to the new Cingular.

A great example of how strategy and execution came together was the expansion of our free mobile-to-mobile calling community. The idea behind the offer was simple: show customers the immediate benefit of being able to call forty-six million people for free. This was the combined number of customers of the two merged companies.

It was important that we be able to advertise immediately that the new Cingular had the largest free mobile-to-mobile calling community in the country. Our IT team embraced the objective completely. Not only did they get the technology in place in time, but they worked out the billing issues on the back end. The instant the companies were combined, former AT&T Wireless customers no longer were billed when they called Cingular customers, and vice versa. Our merger of the networks was virtually flawless. Many customers experienced improved coverage and quality immediately.

A great number of industry experts had predicted that we would lose customers who either would be confused by the merger or frustrated by inevitable glitches. Instead, we had a net gain of 1.7 million customers in the fourth quarter. At the time it was a record for the industry: the largest number of net customer additions for any company, in any quarter, in the history of wireless in the United States.

Building on Momentum

The decision for an accelerated launch anticipated long-term impact.

Sure enough, the trend continued. We gained another five million customers between the end of the fourth quarter of 2004 and the end of the fourth quarter of 2005, and the benefits of the merger can be seen to this day, as you can see from the charts on the next page.

The graph at the lower left refers to operating income before depreciation and amortization. "Churn," which is tracked in the graphic at the lower right, is used to describe customer attrition or loss in the wireless industry.

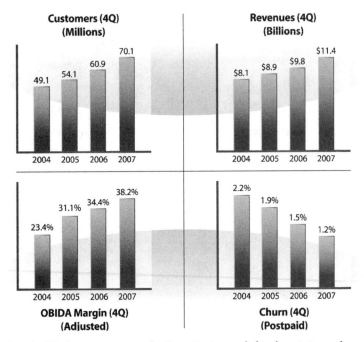

Cingular Wireless post-merger results. Operating income before depreciation and amortization (OBIDA) margin shown on the bottom left-hand chart.

We made the impossible possible. We combined two huge companies in nineteen days. But the real story was about the lasting benefits. Everyone with a stake—customers, the companies and our employees, and shareholders—was substantially better off as a result.

What we accomplished was all the more significant in light of the fact that most mergers and acquisitions fall short of the expected results. Many have started with great fanfare, but ultimately resulted in a clumsy organization that was less than the sum of its parts.

In leading the effort to create the new Cingular through the acquisition of AT&T Wireless, I learned much about successfully integrating big mergers. Based on my experiences at Cingular and my thirty-plus years experience in leading teams, the keys for a successful merger integration are as follows:

- First, establish a clear direction and focus on a select number of success measures. People need a clear direction and confidence that those who set the direction know what they are doing.

- Second, be decisive and establish the top leadership quickly, selecting the best from each company. This solidifies the sense of direction and prevents inertia as people wait to see who lands in what job.

- Third, develop a clear integration plan and focus on executing it well using a program-management approach.

- Fourth, continuously communicate. Be clear, concise, and consistent with your communications. Communication is critical whenever an organization is undergoing significant change. In fact, it's true all the time. But for an undertaking as large as integrating two companies into one, the communication should be especially intense and clear.

- Finally, set high expectations and convey urgency about meeting them. Time after time on my journey, I have seen people surpass everything that seemed reasonable as they strove to fulfill high expectations in pursuit of a vision that gripped them.

Lagniappe and Tarantulas

What makes people buy into a vision? I believe that all of us want to be part of something greater than ourselves. We want to be personally successful. We want to be part of a winning team.

People will do all kinds of extraordinary things to identify with something that really takes hold of them. If you convince people of your vision, they'll want to be a part of the team that makes it happen, and they will go through extraordinary challenges to achieve it.

But managers often fail to understand that. Instead, we tell the people who work with us, "I want you to do this," without explaining why. And so we have talented people doing things without a sense of how they fit into the bigger picture, and it is hard to get their best effort in that situation.

I've always told our salespeople, "Your job isn't to handle an order; your job is to satisfy the customer. Filling the order is part of what you do to please them, but it's really not about the order. Do what it takes to make customers happy."

When you get employees to believe this, great things happen because they'll make an extra effort. They will provide that *lagniappe* (pronounced *lan-yap*), a Creole term I learned when I was running operations in Louisiana. In the old days, people would go to the trading post to buy staples like flour. The shopkeeper would scoop the flour out of a large canvas sack and put it on a scale so the buyer could see that she was getting what she paid for. Once the scale hit a pound, the shopkeeper would add one more scoop as a little extra. This was the lagniappe. I tell our employees, "Give the customer a little lagniappe when you do your job, and they will rave about you."

A lagniappe can be almost any type of "extra." When my family moved to San Antonio after the merger of AT&T and BellSouth, I wanted to have U-verse in our home. U-Verse is a suite of AT&T's Internet-based products and services that includes hi-def television and super-high-speed Internet access. I really wanted to be there for the installation, but I had to be at a meeting that day. So my wife was the one who welcomed the technician.

All day I was eager to hear how the installation went, so that afternoon I called Maria and asked her about the service and how she had been treated by the technician.

"He killed a tarantula," she said.

"What?" I asked. "How about the service? What do you think about it?"

"He killed a tarantula," she said again. "Yes, everything works. But while he was here, he found a huge tarantula and he killed it for me."

That was the technician's lagniappe—and it impressed Maria more than anything else he did. Now, I don't expect all our technicians to go out and kill tarantulas, but my wife just couldn't stop raving about it. You never know what will give a customer that special feeling of appreciation.

That's the vision I want our people to have. I want them to understand that their job is more than just handling an order; it's really to delight the customer. If I plant the idea that this is our purpose, our people will have it in mind when the moment of truth comes, and they will do the right thing.

What All Entrepreneurs Know

People who start and develop companies know all about vision. Successful entrepreneurs are driven by the vision of creating something special. Bill Gates had a vision of putting a computer on every desk. Howard Schultz, the founder of Starbucks, had a vision of creating a third place, somewhere between home and work, where people could feel comfortable and want to come often.

Entrepreneurs like these and hundreds of thousands of others go through incredible hardships and overcome setback after setback, all in an effort to achieve their vision. Their successful visions aren't just about creating *something*. They're about creating a *superlative something*.

Maybe your vision is to have a Tex-Mex restaurant in San Antonio. Or a bakery shop in Wichita. Or to be a blues trumpet player in your own group. Take that vision and broaden it. How about envisioning the *best* restaurant? The *top* bakery shop? The *finest* trumpet player?

Your energy level will go up when your vision is to do something really special. The most successful business leaders have a driving vision that can't be stopped by obstacles.

As I said earlier, I'm a big fan of Junior Achievement, and I try to teach JA classes as often as I can. Not long ago, I talked to a class about entrepreneurship. The lecture included the use of cards—like baseball cards—that showed some of the country's greatest entrepreneurs.

We used the cards to talk about entrepreneurship, and I wasn't sure the kids were connecting with these big-name entrepreneurs. So I asked them what their parents did for a living. Then it became clear that some of these kids came from entrepreneurial families, but they had never realized it. This boy's dad owned a restaurant. That girl's mother had a greeting card store.

Well, those parents are entrepreneurs.

All of a sudden it began to kick in that they are no strangers to entrepreneurs. They started to think, *Even if I'm a teenager, I can be an entrepreneur; I can start my own company.* It doesn't have to be the biggest in the world as long as the vision is to be extraordinary.

Once you get the bug to create something new, it's infectious. Two or three people want to join you, and great things start to happen. And it grows from there. This is why we teach the kids in JA about financial literacy, entrepreneurship, and workforce readiness, so that they can become inspired to create their own vision and pursue their own dreams.

Getting Buy-In and Spreading the Word

In creating the vision for an organization, you want to get everyone involved. People simply work harder toward a goal that they had a say in bringing to life.

When we changed the vision for the new AT&T, many

people had significant input. The business had always been about connecting people. Originally that meant voice communications from one phone to another. Over time it became much more. Today, we connect people to their world. To their world of business, to their world of entertainment, to whatever in the world is important to them personally.

And so our new vision is more expansive than anything that telecoms companies once envisioned—to help connect you to your world, and to do it better than anyone else. To deliver on this vision, we must to be more customer-centric than ever. We need to understand what your world looks like, what you want to connect to, and how you want to do it. From now on, the answers to these questions define our business.

The critical point is to keep asking the questions, and be ready for fresh answers. This is how you make sure that what you're trying to accomplish actually aligns with your vision.

For an entrepreneur, the communication of the vision needs to captivate different stakeholder groups. It has to sell investors on the prospect of above-average ROI, potential employees on the idea of work that is personally and financially rewarding, and customers on a value proposition that stands out from the crowd.

When I was at BellSouth, there was a favorite acronym that reminded us constantly about the vision we needed to communicate. The bottom-line concern of each shareholder, worker, and customer was always WIIFM: "What's in it for me?" The more personal you make the WIIFM, the better. For example, a sales team focused on WIIFM would think of competitors as taking food off their families' tables. The way they could prevent that is through the fulfillment of the vision.

Once in a Lifetime

At AT&T when we launched our TV service (U-Verse), I gave a speech to the new employees we were hiring. I told them they were about to experience a once-in-a-life opportunity. We were putting our new technology up against tough, entrenched competition. They would be at the vanguard of a completely different way to connect customers with the entertainment they desired. One day, they would tell their grandchildren about being the pioneers of a technological revolution. So this was more than just a job. This was history.

People get excited about a vision that invites them to become part of history—as long as they believe that you, the vision owner, are excited right along with them.

Steady Commitment

If you've developed the vision in the right way, it's not going to change every thirty days. It will be consistent. Adjustments are to be expected. In fact, they are essential because the world itself changes. But if the changes are significant, and if they come too often, people will lose faith. They will stop paying attention.

Big organizations constantly fight the "program du jour"

syndrome. An initiative is launched with a lot of fanfare. Then the changes start. Before long, the initiative has run out of steam. Progress dies as people quit taking it seriously.

Sacrifice

My last word on vision is a reminder of the sacrifice it takes. Today's world is flat, and by that I mean that competition comes from all corners. Innovations are copied almost as fast as they hit the market.

A great idea—and early success with it—rarely means you can put your feet up and relax. Stop working, stop innovating, and the market will be swamped by your idea made overseas at half the cost. Be prepared for the reality that it takes as much energy to sustain a vision as to create and launch it.

This country of ours was shaped by people willing to make huge sacrifices. Recently in New York I visited the Ellis Island Museum and was deeply moved by the powerful stories. In Key West, I have visited the Cuban Transit Home and Museum, which displays some of the tiny boats, homemade rafts, and even inner tubes that have been used to attempt the ninety-mile crossing from Cuba to Florida.

Sacrifice for the sake of a vision is part of our culture, but unfortunately it's easy to forget the hardships after a while and take the success for granted. Have we gotten soft and become too accustomed to the good life? Maybe. But every day, entrepreneurs with a vision still put everything on the line and make the sacrifices that lead to new products, jobs, breakthroughs, and possibilities for Americans and the world.

Your Personal Vision

Everyone needs a personal vision. It doesn't have to be a formal one. And it doesn't have to be detailed, as long as you can internalize it to keep it alive day by day.

I have seen people who carry a little card with their vision on it. Others carry an image in their heads—the day their book is going to be published, or opening day at their restaurant, or taking off on the trip they've always dreamed of. Whether you write it down or keep it in your head, put your vision at the forefront of your efforts. Focus on it. Keep it clear in your mind.

And how do you know what your vision is? When you can't wait to work on a particular something, when you can't stop talking about it, when you wake up and go to sleep thinking about how to make it happen, then you've found your vision.

Takeaway messages

It starts with vision. Your vision should drive everything you do.

Get people's buy-in. A vision is just a theoretical exercise unless people want to be a part of it because you have made it exciting and compelling.

Sacrifice is key. If you truly are going to accomplish something great, it will take sacrifice. Expect it. Embrace it.

SIX

The Only Way to Win

During my first week as a Southern Bell engineer, right out of college, my integrity was challenged. This was the 1970s, and public telephones were still a big part of our business. Management trainees like me were assigned a certain number of pay phones to monitor as part of our job. This involved checking to see they had Yellow Pages, making sure the booth was clean, and testing the phone to confirm that it worked. The test involved placing a call.

The first pay phone I tested gave me a surprise. When I put my coin in, the change inside the phone came gushing out. It was like hitting three bananas on a Las Vegas slot machine. This was my first week on the job, and I could have used the money since I hadn't yet received a paycheck. But I turned in the cache of coins to my district manager and told him what had happened. That was the last I thought of it.

A couple of days later, he came over to me and said, "Son, did you know those coins were marked?" I had no idea what he meant. As it turned out, he told me the company frequently marked coins with invisible ink as an honesty test for coin collectors. "If you hadn't turned them in, we probably would have fired you," he told me.

Thank God I did the right thing and turned in every one of those coins. It was a heck of a lesson for my first week on the job. I returned the coins because it was the right thing to do. But the episode also taught me that integrity is not just the *right* thing to do; it's the *wise* thing as well.

Everything Communicates

As I rose in management, I came to realize an important truth. The people I supervised were very sensitive to whether even small details of my actions matched my words. If I preached to our technicians about wearing safety glasses in the field, I had better do the same when riding with them. Everything about a manager's behavior communicates. Little disconnects erode respect and loyalty.

Companies invest tens of millions to communicate carefully crafted messages about their brand. Consistency and repetition are paramount. When Cingular and AT&T Wireless merged as Cingular Wireless, our rebranding effort, as you just saw, took every nuance into account. We weren't going to allow any deviation that could blur the sharp and clear identity we wanted to build.

It's the same in management. As a leader, you become your own brand. People associate certain attributes with you based on how you conduct yourself. Owning the attribute of authenticity depends on adhering to the same standards you hold up for your people.

Young managers don't always appreciate this fact. It wasn't on my radar screen until I had been in management for a while. Since I realized it, the lesson has been in the middle of my radar screen.

WorldCom was a company that lost its way. Enron was even more high-profile. The early 2000s were a bleak era in terms of well-publicized ethical lapses by some executives and companies. On the one hand, we saw that shedding the demands of integrity doesn't necessarily block short-term success. In fact, it sometimes accelerates it if only certain quantitative measures are used. On the other hand, the eventual destruction in ruined lives, devastated families, betrayed employees, and collateral damage is beyond measure. In the case of Enron, thousands of its employees lost their jobs and their retirement savings, stockholders found their holdings suddenly worthless, and some of the top execs landed in prison.

Pyramid of Principles

When I think about the values and actions needed to succeed in the right way, they form what I call the Pyramid of Principles. It's a bottom-up model.

Integrity and credibility form the base upon which everything else rests. Each time I start a new assignment, I gather my team and go through this pyramid. It is vital that they understand it as the model for how we will operate.

Emphasizing the pyramid up front gets everyone on the same page about how the organization will operate. The time I spent with BellSouth Latin America drove home the importance of doing this. We were a U.S.-owned business operating in multiple international markets. The culture was different, as was the language. So I always had a "values conversation" with my direct reports, and their direct reports, and went over the Pyramid of Principles. Otherwise, given the different systems of government and local traditions, our people could have carried out orders in a way that would be okay locally but inconsistent with U.S. laws.

As a leader using the principles of the pyramid, it's important to remember that you set the tone (the tone at the top) by how you behave and what you communicate. People sometimes interpret small things as big signals when they are nothing of the sort.

I learned this when Cingular and AT&T Wireless were being integrated. Cingular's headquarters was in Atlanta, and the wireless business of AT&T was based in Redmond, Washington. The plan was for the post-merger company to be headquartered in Atlanta, and this had been announced to our people. But a rumor got started that we were thinking of relocating some functions in Redmond. It started after I returned from spending three days in Redmond and made some comments to the effect that it was really a very nice area. This quickly morphed into an undercurrent about plans to relocate some functions there. But back to the pyramid . . .

The Foundation: Integrity and Credibility

In the Pyramid of Principles, integrity and credibility provide the stability. Let's look at these blocks more closely.

Many of the key episodes of my career have involved projects in which the goals were very ambitious. In these situations, it is a leader's responsibility to emphasize integrity as an essential part of the effort, right along with the goals and objectives. Yes, we're aiming high, but we're aiming straight as well. I believe that anyone who has worked with me has always understood that I prize integrity *and* results, fully linked together.

One of my first key executive assignments involved assuming leadership of an organization that had low morale because previous management had not upheld the company's values. When I took over the group, employees were concerned about further shake-ups and job security. Self-protection was the top priority. While the impulse was perhaps understandable, the consequences of their mind-set were unacceptable to the business. Often when I would ask someone to do something, he or she wanted me to put it in writing to create a paper record of justification—an absurd waste of time that would only deepen the culture of fear. It took a long time to reestablish trust and get the organization focused on effectiveness rather than on waiting for the next shoe to drop. Eventually, I convinced them that I wouldn't have been chosen for the job if my trustworthiness were in doubt.

Credibility is closely related to integrity. Credibility is about winning the confidence of others that your word is good; it's doing what you said you were going to do. Those who work with you must have no doubt that you will do the right thing whether anyone is looking or not. For a leader, credibility is an invaluable personal asset. Put into consistent practice, it becomes an organizational asset as well.

Here's a hypothetical example. Suppose the billing department of a company discovers it has mistakenly overcharged one thousand customers three dollars each. On the one hand, the administrative cost of correcting the error will exceed the amount of the overcharge. What's more, there is no way these customers would ever realize that they have wrongly lost three dollars. Giving them notification and crediting their next bill for three dollars isn't going to buy much goodwill. Is it really worth all the effort?

Yes—because it reinforces the foundation of the pyramid. The company's sense of right and wrong, as well as its sense of duty to customers, grows stronger by doing the right thing. Integrity and credibility are fortified internally as well as externally. And that alone is worth the cost of fixing the mistake.

Let me give you a real example. I was leading an aggressive effort for our organization to make our annual plan. We were all pulling together, and things were going well, but two months before our deadline, a major error was uncovered in the way our results were being calculated. We thought we had more subscribers than was actually the case. Correcting the mistake would put our annual goals in jeopardy. It was a jolt, to say the least!

We could ignore the error and continue as though nothing had happened, or we could correct how we were calculating our results and figure out a way to still hit our goals. I made the course correction immediately. We corrected the way we did the calculation. In the end, our team did deliver on our commitments, but more importantly, we grew stronger as a team. In the end, we learned that we could accomplish even more than we had thought possible. And the foundation of the pyramid was reinforced for each of us.

Integrity and credibility are not "sometimes" attributes. They require consistency. We are all human beings and make human mistakes, like missing a deadline. If this occurs once in a blue moon, there's no harm done. But if it's a regular occurrence, credibility starts to diminish, and your reputation suffers irreparable harm. It's like a receiver in football who sometimes makes a great catch but can't be counted on for the routine plays. I'm not going to build my team around him.

Teamwork

When putting together your team, you need people who bring the requisite skills to get the job done and who have a terrific attitude. It is not either/or. You want great skills and a great attitude. It's not one or the other; it's both that put you at the peak of performance.

In addition to assembling the right mix of skills and talents, I want my team to reflect the customer base we are going to serve. If you have product that is used 50 percent by women, how could you *not* have a good representation of females on the team to advise on how that product is used, how to make it better, what features should be added? Although this is common sense, it is surprising how often companies try to design products and services without having a representative view of the customer base. We will talk more about this later.

Once you have the right mix of people, how well they work together is largely up to you as the leader. It's like the role of a coach in a team sport. You need to make sure all team members are clear on what they need to accomplish, both individually and collectively. When you see someone lagging behind, you provide immediate coaching.

Not everyone who can help you succeed is a team player in the way that phrase is usually applied. Some very talented people work best on their own rather than in collaborative activities. This is often true of individuals with highly developed specialties of a technical nature. So, again like a sports coach, you find the position and situation in which that individual can shine. Never try to force people to work against their own strengths. Put them in the best position to do their best work.

Attitude

Which brings me to the subject of attitude. What do I mean by the right attitude? I am not talking being cheery and pleasant (although no one wants to work with a grouch). By the right attitude, I mean people who are focused on the right goals and who have a relentless commitment to accomplishing them. The tougher the assignment, the more fiercely dedicated they become.

When we set the goal at Cingular Wireless to have the new company up and running nineteen days after the merger with AT&T Wireless, it was a huge stretch objective. The galvanizing effect it had on our people was incredible. Everybody was sky high and determined to do everything within his or her power to push us closer to the goal. The fact that it was risky added to the excitement. My guess is that even today, those involved would say it was one of the most exhilarating times in their career—as well as quite possibly the most demanding. Pulling it off, we felt like champions. And the truth is, that's exactly what we were; we had the best quarter of any company in the history of wireless.

For my team, I want people like these who want the bar set high. They desire to stretch themselves and be part of a group working on something truly challenging. When such individuals realize they are part of a truly exceptional achievement, their can-do attitude builds internal momentum in the organization. It becomes contagious.

To see the right attitude in action, look for persistence and open-mindedness when it comes to solving difficult problems. Talking over a difficult task with people is a good way to take the measure of their attitude. If they tell you the thing can't be done, keep looking for other team members. If they say they'll find a way to figure it out, you've chosen wisely.

Excellence and Vision

"I believe that this nation should commit itself to the goal, before this decade is out, of landing a man on the moon and returning him safely to Earth."

When President John F. Kennedy declared those words to the American people in May 1961, he created one of the greatest visions of the twentieth century. Talk about the power of a clearly communicated vision!

Looking back, it still seems impossible that such a bold and unprecedented objective could be achieved in less than ten years. But once America became intensely focused on this goal, no obstacle was too big to overcome. Thousands of men and women of excellence and vision were directly involved. NASA had over two hundred thousand engineers and project managers on the Mercury, Gemini, and Apollo missions. When astronaut Neil Armstrong became the first man to walk on the moon on July 20, 1969, the impossible had been achieved—once again!

Excellence is not an abstract idea to me. That is why the pyramid is completed with the principles of excellence and vision. Those words describe a person who sets stretch goals, drives for results in the right way (grounded in integrity), and outperforms the competition. Such people are the most valuable resource an organization can have. They equate personal success with team success, especially if they are in a leadership position. They are quick to credit colleagues and subordinates. For these individuals, winning is always about *us*.

Vision crowns the pyramid. I've already had a lot to say about the importance of a compelling vision, so its lofty position in the pyramid shouldn't come as a surprise. People respond to an ambitious vision. They want to be part of it, to support it, to sacrifice for it, and to rejoice in its accomplishment.

What If You Are Tomorrow's Headline?

It doesn't take more than a glance at the headlines to see that some leaders try to win using models very different from the Pyramid of Principles. These individuals lost sight of the fact that the *how* matters as much as the goal itself.

Your own pyramid may look slightly different from mine. What matters is that you base your actions on a set of beliefs, values, or characteristics that define who you are. Some people like to work off of a personal mission statement. A good start would be something along the lines of, "I'm going to live my life and handle my business so that I won't be ashamed if it's printed on the front page of tomorrow's newspaper."

Whatever you put in your personal mission statement, just remember there is only one way to win—with credibility grounded in integrity that never wavers.

Takeaway Messages

As individuals, and as members of organizations, we need a set of values on which everything rests. Mine take the form of a pyramid, the Pyramid of Principles.

Integrity—Being a leader means being honest and ethical—and insisting on the same from every member of your team. Even the smallest of failures in integrity cause cracks in the moral foundation of the organization.

Credibility—If you want to be respected, you must (at the very least) do what you said you were going to do.

Teamwork—Business is not an individual sport; it's a team sport. If you can get teams of people to work together, you can do incredible things. But you also have to leave room for contributions by those who work best alone.

Attitude—I have not found a better predictor of a person's success than attitude. There is no future in believing things can't be done. The future is in making them happen!

Excellence—You want people who always are trying to be better than they were the day before.

Vision—People need clarity about what you are trying to accomplish. They must see your vision and help others to see it, internalize it, and believe in it.

SEVEN

Life's a Journey—
Prepare for the Trip

Many years ago, I met a bright woman who had been an executive assistant. While there were important responsibilities in her job, this woman clearly had managerial potential. She recognized this fact, as did some of us who knew her. I encouraged her to prepare for a bigger job by going back to school. First she got her bachelor's degree. Then she went on to get an MBA.

Even so, nothing really changed for her. She was ready for bigger responsibilities, but unfortunately she continued to be viewed in her old role. Realizing this was not going to change, she found a very good job with a different company that welcomed her for her credentials, rather than penalizing her based on the past. Her old company was the loser for failing to see her potential as clearly as she did.

Who's in Control?

A few people on this earth just seem destined to enjoy success. Things appear to work out for them naturally, with very little effort. These people are extremely rare, and the odds of being one of them are too small to take seriously.

For the other 99.99 percent of us, such as the MBA-earner just described, achieving the success we want doesn't come so easy. It takes a lot of work in our personal life and on the job.

The good news is, the effort pays off. Leadership can be learned. Success can be won. Each of us is in control of our own journey—deciding where we want to go, and how to get there.

The following graphic, adapted from David A. Kolb's *Experiential Learning,* shows how this happens as life experiences combine with education, work, and personal development to shape the capacity to lead.[1]

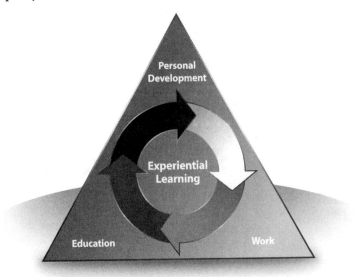

If you have the desire to be a leader and are willing to work at developing the necessary skills, you can make it happen. Yet many people who have this desire still fall short. It's not because they don't put in the work. Rather, they don't dream big enough, and wind up settling for being less than they could become.

Breaking Chains

Why would someone with energy, ability, and ambition choose to set his or her sights too low? It might reflect a mind-set of limits that was formed while growing up. At the circus, notice the elephants. All it takes to keep the largest land creature on earth under control is a small chain around one leg. A fully grown elephant easily could break the chain but instead accepts it without a struggle. Why is this? At an early age, when the small elephant is not strong enough to break free, the chain becomes part of its sense of reality. Years later, the chain's power still works over the elephant's mind, and therefore over its body as well.

In a similar way, many capable people allow themselves to be confined by a sense of being limited that they formed as children. Let's say a teenager is the first member of the family to go to college. Even though his GPA and test scores indicate that he could handle academic work at top schools, he doesn't apply to them and instead attends a good-but-not-great college. He is not ready to make a dramatic departure from the impressions of his youth.

Another reason people may aim below their potential is that they are encouraged to do so by others. It seems to be human nature to categorize and put each other in boxes. If you dream big, there will be people who doubt you can make the dream happen . . . or resent you for shooting so high. You may detect a muted reaction of *Who do you think you are?* This attitude can chip away at your confidence and conviction if you allow it to. That's entirely up to you.

If you feel underutilized in your current situation, change it! If your boss has treated you in a way that cuts off exciting possibilities you want to pursue, find a new boss. That's a tough message, I know. But when someone stands in the way of your dreams, drastic action may be called for to get past the obstacle. Otherwise, you could stop believing in your dream or yourself, merely accepting the verdict of others about who you are and what you can be.

George Bernard Shaw captured the idea I want to get across here: *Some men see things as they are and ask why? I dream of things that never were and ask why not?*

Dream your future—and then ask, "Why not?"

Who Is a Leader Anyway?

Big dreams usually involve being in a leadership role. In the context of an organization, leadership means motivating people to achieve things above and beyond the norm, sometimes things they thought were impossible. Think of entrepreneurs like Steve Jobs of Apple who have built an industry from an idea. Or think of executives who totally re-created a huge, entrenched company—like Jack Welch did at General Electric.

Then there's another type of leader: the individual pioneer working in a particular field who pushes back boundaries and creates something new and valuable. This kind of leader may work alone, for the most part, perhaps as an artist, a writer, a scientist, or a brilliant software developer. Such work has the power to touch and change millions of people.

Leadership is an expansive concept, embracing both traditional and nontraditional ways of having an impact on others. It is flexible enough to fit many situations, but there are a couple of common denominators in all of them. One is the commitment of the leader to do a thing to the very best of his or her ability. The other is the outcome: directly or indirectly, others will be influenced and inspired.

Preparing for Leadership

In the 1980s, I enrolled in the MBA program at Northern Illinois University. Getting my MBA, with all of my demanding responsibilities leading the analog-to-digital transformation at Bellcore, was extremely challenging. I went to school at nights and on weekends. Between the work and the studies, there was little time with my family. What kept me going were the doors I knew would open to me, and the steadfast support of my wife, Maria.

I often look back at those days and wonder how I managed to pull it off. Once when I was on a plane, I was trying to study. I kept pulling books out of my briefcase and carry-on bag. At one point I had so many of them out that the person next to me asked me if I was a book editor. But at this point in my career, I knew that my desired destination mandated getting an MBA. So that's where I steered my life.

The majority of people we recognize for great leadership have deliberately put themselves in position to learn from a breadth of experiences. They have sought out assignments and training, such as my MBA, that expose them to new challenges and problem-solving opportunities.

In the top ranks of Fortune 500 companies, you will find CEOs who came up through the ranks from all kinds of starting points. Sales, marketing, accounting, human resources, legal, production . . . even some from engineering! But no matter what field they started in, take a look at the rest of the résumé. Invariably you will see that these future leaders branched out into different functional areas. They shaped themselves for leadership by making sure they had a range of professional experiences outside their original discipline.

Also, they volunteered for difficult assignments, taking on the kind of responsibilities that teach and took them outside of their comfort zone. You can't always plan these assignments (hurricanes, for example). But some *are* a matter of purposeful targeting, for the very reason that they are difficult. Taking the presidency of BellSouth Latin America is an example from my own career. I accepted this assignment knowing that it would be a pivotal learning experience as well as a rare opportunity to make a difference for the company by turning around a challenging situation.

Defeating the "Yes, Buts"

There is one more common trait you will find in the career paths of leaders. Through their years on the rise, they take care to fill gaps in their qualifications—so that when one of their names comes up at a key moment for a desirable opportunity, there is no obvious cause for someone to say, "Yes, but . . ."

"Yes, she's good . . . but no international experience."

"Yes, he's got what it takes . . . but no MBA."

Those are two of the most common "yes, buts" in today's business world. Every industry, every company, has some of its own. If you work in a chemical company, you might need a PhD to climb the ladder. If you work for a global manufacturer, you can't spend your whole career in the United States and expect to reach the top. It will take operational experience in different markets.

Make sure you understand the requirements that apply in your world, and take them very seriously. If you aren't sure, ask the boss—or the boss's boss. Then map out and follow a plan for removing every "yes, but" that could knock you off course.

Sometimes I hear people express the opinion that too much emphasis is placed on an MBA, that it's really just a "box check-off." I disagree strongly. Let me tell you what having an MBA communicates to others.

If I'm looking at a candidate to take on a stretch assignment, an MBA tells me that the individual: is disciplined; is willing to pay the price to achieve a goal; has a solid financial education (sometimes lacking in employees with only an undergraduate degree); and has gained meaningful knowledge about a breadth of business functions. In short, merely having an MBA answers a number of important questions. Many of the potential "yes, buts" automatically go away.

Let me give you another example of eliminating the "yes, buts." Coming out of engineering school, I was not trained as a public speaker. But in a big company, the ability to communicate clearly and effectively to large groups is very definitely an element of leadership.

This was a gap I needed to address. So I joined the company's speakers' bureau, which sent representatives out to civic groups and community organizations to make presentations about our business. Through the speakers' bureau I received constructive criticism and got a lot of practice. Not only did my delivery improve; I came to enjoy public speaking and feel confident about it. I developed the ability to be quick on my feet if something went off-script. This was extremely helpful in Latin America as I was working to win over a room of doubtful country executives to the more unified, collaborative approach we were implementing.

It also was helpful much earlier in my career, when a challenge came out of left field from one of my employees. When I was BellSouth operations manager for North Dade County in Florida, I was eager for our team to have an outstanding United Way drive. So I arranged with work-center managers and officials from the Communications Workers of America to set up breakfasts to rally the troops. I went to each breakfast and made a short speech.

Having gone to high school in Hialeah, Florida, North Dade County was my home turf. At one of the work centers, a man raised his hand after I spoke. He was an outside plant technician, which is a physically demanding job. Standing up, he was well over six feet tall and very imposing. His question was like none I had ever heard, and haven't heard since. "Hey, didn't I know you in high school, and didn't I beat you up one time?"

The room became very quiet. I looked at him and answered, "Didn't I cut you?" Everyone broke up in laughter. They got the fact that I had been raised in a mixed, inner-city neighborhood and knew how to take care of myself. People talk, and word of this exchange made the rounds to other work centers. We went on to have one of our best United Way drives ever, and I don't think it was a coincidence.

In time I came to know the technician very well, and it turned out we had never had a confrontation in high school. But even if we had, I would have appreciated the opportunity it afforded me to make a connection with my employees. Public speaking, which had been a noticeable gap in my skill set, became something that actually became an asset in my career once I mastered it.

No Shortcuts

Recently I got an e-mail that I wanted to print and frame. It came from an employee who, some years ago, had asked me for career advice. My suggestion had been that he finish his degree. He listened and acted.

Not only did this man earn a BS in business; he graduated

summa cum laude and then entered an executive MBA program at the University of Miami. In the e-mail he informed me that he was about to graduate at the top of his MBA class. He was writing "to express my gratitude for the advice you bestowed and the significant impact you had on me that day. Thank you for making such a difference in my life."

Not only has this young man done well for himself; he has a very responsible position with our company. Reading his message was a very gratifying moment for me.

I gave the advice, but he did the work. Many people can see the footprints that lead to the top, but they don't like the path. It's too hard. Too time-consuming. So they try shortcuts. That's a bad choice, almost every time.

If you want to become a leader, the worst path to try is the quick one. That path skips over too much valuable learning, and your reputation and credibility wind up suffering. All that you've done to build up your reputation and credibility can be lost in a hurry if you are perceived as taking shortcuts. The odds of failure go way up.

There are valuable, and easy, ways to prepare yourself for leadership beyond the learning that comes from job assignments. One is to apply to your own field of responsibility the experiences you have had as a consumer. "Is this how I would want to be treated?" "Does anything feel wrong about taking this action?" "What feels right?"

Reading widely is another way of expanding your contact with different types of learning experiences. Jack Welch is one of my favorite executive authors. John Kotter is very good on leadership behavior. Jim Collins made my short list of preferred authors when I read *Good to Great* and *Built to Last.*

If reading is a chore, don't feel that you have to pore over every sentence. Skip around, looking for topics that have special relevance for you. It might be that just one terrific chapter makes you glad you picked up an otherwise forgettable book. Take the best, leave the rest.

Leader of the Pack

My family just got a new puppy, a sheltie named Brandy. This event coincides with a sudden surge of interest on my part in the TV show *The Dog Whisperer,* in which Cesar Millan shows owners how to transform even the worst-behaving dog into a model member of the household.

One of Millan's key principles is that to your dog, you and he/she comprise a pack. Your dog needs to see you as the pack leader. Everything hinges on this. The dog wants you to take charge and show leadership, and if you don't, the result for the dog is confusion that results in misbehavior.

Millan's ability to communicate his leadership to dogs is stunning. Within minutes, a dog that has been highly dysfunctional is minding in a way that amazes the owners. They never dreamed it was possible.

People are obviously not dogs. But they are very similar in one way: in the absence of leadership in an organization, their behavior can become dysfunctional and destructive.

I am convinced that the same is true for the individual in his or her own life. In Junior Achievement I have come to know an author and fellow board member named Susan Butler. Susan has written a book called *Become the CEO of You Inc.* To me, that's a powerful way to describe the maturity, vision, and effort required to take charge of your life and your dreams.

Leadership starts with you taking charge of *you.*

Takeaway Messages

Leadership is a learned skill for most people.

Dreaming big makes you more likely to succeed as long as you match your dreams with hard work.

Only you can allow limits to be imposed on your dreams.

It's up to you to **understand the "yes-but" factors** in your field, and remove them from your path.

On the path to leadership, avoid shortcuts, because **nothing can substitute for experience and learning**.

EIGHT

The Success Cycle

It's one thing to say you want to be successful. It is quite another to have a plan for assuring that you are successful. Without a plan, it is *possible* you could succeed. You *could* get lucky. Things *might* go your way by accident. But the odds are not in your favor.

Instead of leaving things to chance, I want to be in the driver's seat on my life's journey. If you want to do the same—and be successful at it—then you must follow the *success cycle*. This cycle has five stages.

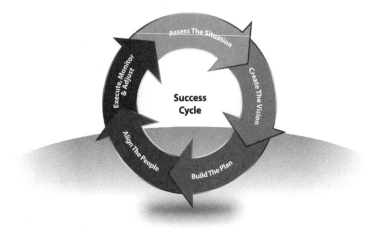

Phase One—Assess the Situation

As a ten-year-old boy separated from my parents and family, living in a strange place where I didn't know the language, had no money, and didn't like the food, there were plenty of negatives to dwell on. It would have been easy to feel helpless and victimized by forces beyond my control.

But was I helpless? Not at all. Even at a young age, I could see that the positives of my situation were just as powerful as the negatives. I was living in the greatest country on the planet, the United States of America. I had two wonderful surrogate parents, Ada and Arnaldo Baez, who treated me as if I were their own child. I also had the example of courage that my own parents had shown, first in being willing to leave Cuba, and then in sending me on alone. With all of these factors working for me, I became determined to succeed.

The starting point of the success cycle is a frank and honest appraisal of whatever situation you are facing. I call this phase "facing the brutal facts."

This doesn't mean just dwelling on negatives. Along with being honest about the obstacles and limitations you might confront, it's important to give just as much attention to the possibilities.

You are not a victim unless you allow yourself to be paralyzed by whatever is difficult about your life. The other choice is to direct your energies toward the opportunities inherent in your situation. It's up to you, always.

Phase Two—Create the Vision

Having assessed the situation, it's time to define what success looks like to you. This is a highly personal picture of the life you want to create. Only you can create this picture—your vision of life's ideal journey.

Sometimes events force your hand—such as an urgent situation that requires immediate action. But the longer you wait to articulate a vision of where you are going, the more out of alignment things get. You could find yourself having to double back to make sure you are heading toward the destination that makes the most sense. That's the last thing you want to do, especially if your competition is forging ahead.

Phase Three—Build the Plan

With your vision established, it's time to take concrete steps to achieve it. One of my favorite sayings is "Hope is not a strategy." First comes planning, and then actions based on your plan to move you toward your vision.

So in this third phase of the success cycle, you identify the strategies or key initiatives required to achieve the vision. A sound plan will highlight your top priorities and assign accountability for making them happen. (Of course, if this is a personal plan, all the accountabilities are your own.)

Be clear and focused. In planning for an organization, clarity and focus are paramount. Ambiguities can lead to uncertainty or misalignment, ultimately causing poor results.

Be concise. How many thick, wordy plans in three-ring binders wind up gathering dust on somebody's shelf, never read? Plans are unlikely to be taken seriously unless they are succinct, direct, and very clear about objectives, accountabilities, approaches, and outcomes.

Get input from your team. Good organizational planning is never done in a vacuum. Your team members need to feel ownership for the final product. Remember, you will be asking them to give their very best. So first, ask them to give their ideas and opinions. Getting quality input will take time and effort. People will disagree, often vehemently. But it has to be done.

My experience in Latin America illustrates the point. We really needed to take advantage of the scope and scale of our eleven country markets, which previously had operated as independent business units. But each one was used to doing its own thing. They all located and purchased their own handsets, hired their own ad agencies, did their own promotions. This led to a lot of mixed messages to our customers. "Free nights and weekends" would be featured in ads in one country, while in another country we emphasized basic plans with more minutes.

We lacked the consistency that is necessary for building a strong brand.

The whole approach was inefficient. Take purchasing, for example. How could a small market like Uruguay cut the high cost of handsets? The same way you and I cut costs when we shop at wholesale clubs: we buy in bulk to get overall savings. By leveraging the buying power of much larger markets, like Argentina and Brazil, we could buy handsets in bigger numbers. But instead, we had eleven businesses, each going its own way shopping on its own.

The solution was clear. We needed a plan for operating all eleven countries as one business, while giving the country chief executives sufficient flexibility to address local market conditions. But getting to this point meant that everyone had to agree on some key matters, and it wasn't happening. Take phone features, for example. Each country's representatives insisted on the criticality of features that were unique to its market. No one was giving an inch!

In a situation like this, the leader can simply impose a decision. But if you do that, you run the risk of passive resistance, which can undermine a plan just as surely as overt opposition. So I felt it would be counterproductive to unilaterally announce, "Here are the phones that every country will sell," or "Everyone will follow this one-size-fits-all Mother's Day promotion." But it was tempting!

Seeing things from their point of view, I realized that these executives genuinely believed that the best interests of the business depended on maintaining country-by-country autonomy. They had never operated collaboratively before and didn't have a clear view of how it would work. They were smart, capable people who knew their markets and had lots of operational experience that I valued. Winning them over to a new mind-set was important because we needed their experience and talent to grow the business.

As I described earlier, we held a summit meeting to find common ground. Not surprisingly, during the first part of the meeting all I heard was how Latin America was different from the rest of the world. Many reasons were given about why the region could not be operated as one big business unit. I listened and took notes. Then I told them I was going to play back to them all the reasons they had told me that unifying the eleven markets was impossible. Unstable political situations . . . crashing economies . . . different cultures . . . the loan default by a partnership . . . and a number of other negative factors. Then I turned these negatives around to say, "With all of these threats and obstacles, it is more important than ever for us to come together and maximize our combined strength."

Eventually, they got it. They realized that emerging global competition would make it difficult to win in the marketplace if we could not unite and leverage our scale. Once a common vision and consensus around a plan was developed, we were able to move ahead and make tremendous strides. We started with a compelling vision of being part of something bigger and bolder than the present state of our business. What was BellSouth Latin America's vision? *To be the leading wireless communications provider in our Latin America markets.*

Having established the vision, we identified the key strategic imperatives necessary to turn it into a reality:

- Grow revenues

- Retain customer base

- Improve profitability

- Develop best in class leadership

- Generate positive cash flow

Notice that there were only five key imperatives (must do's). We were very focused. With these imperatives identified, we set out to develop tactics to execute the strategies. We didn't set out to do one thousand things—just a few. Coming up with them took time and energy. There were debates, which were totally necessary for everyone to buy in.

Once we had settled on the operating plan, I told everyone at the summit, "I want your signature to show that you have bought into this plan and we're now going to operate as one. This is our declaration that we are going to work together—just like the Declaration of Independence, which brought the United States together. We're going to depend on each other to succeed. We are going to win as a united team."

The process of building consensus around that plan started us on the path of becoming one company. It was a key moment of learning for me. Initially, I had wanted to plunge in and attack all the problems we had in Latin America. But I realized that even though things were crazy and the problems were huge, if I couldn't get the people who would be executing the plan to feel that they owned it, nothing good was going to happen. If they didn't feel it was their plan, it just wasn't going to work.

Today I believe that this approach is the only way to shape an organization that will be successful for the long term. To get real buy-in, you have to give people a chance to speak their minds and object to the things they don't like. You absolutely want them to push back. You want to hear them out and adopt their best ideas. Only then can you move forward with momentum.

It's interesting to see how team members embrace the end results of this process, even if they had doubts at the start. Because you listened to them, because they had a say in shaping the vision and plan, most of them will become supporters. This is true, even though they probably don't get everything they wanted.

As positive results begin to flow in, the support solidifies. In Latin America we started selling a common set of cell phones across all countries of the region. The competitive advantages were clear—state-of-the-art handsets that cost dramatically less because of our procurement scale. But it was the process of reaching this point, not the phones themselves, that made our country executives advocates of unified planning and teamwork.

We built the plan, kept it concise, and used input from all the team members.

Phase Four—Align the People

Communicating the plan must go beyond the executive level out into the ranks of the company. The whole organization needs to become aligned with top priorities and operational goals. Managers must be clear with subordinates on who is responsible for what aspects of execution. Everyone needs to know what is expected of whom. Ideally the plan looks out three years, so resources and funding can be properly planned and brought to bear in plenty of time.

Obtaining funding can be extremely frustrating, especially if you know you have a truly wonderful idea. But the fact is it's the company's capital. Others have wonderful ideas too. Senior management has an obligation to make sure that capital is spent wisely and generates a good return, and just doesn't go to fund the pet project of the squeakiest wheel or more persuasive executive. Entrepreneurs go through the same process to convince venture capitalists to give them money. They have to sell their ideas to a prospective investor or lender, much as someone at AT&T Mobility needs to sell an idea to me.

Let me make a point that may surprise you: when you are in the selling mode, you may not be setting your goals high enough. In my experience, people don't always think as big as their idea really is. They don't stretch themselves or their organizations enough. Instead of trying to do dramatically better, they settle for the incremental. I like to see plans that set stretch targets and move us to industry leadership. This should be your mind-set. What will it take to be the best? It is incumbent upon everyone—employees and leaders—to think that way.

For example, if you tell me you need more people, I don't have any problem with that as long as you can show me how revenue and profits will grow as a result of their efforts. Commit to achieving those results, and I'll gladly authorize more people for your organization.

At AT&T Mobility, we did this in 2007 in our retail organization. We hired more people for our stores to push sales and service levels higher. It worked. We set an industry record for net customer additions and delivered the best one-quarter sales and margins in our company's history.

Phase Five—Execute, Monitor, and Adjust

A good plan is a living instrument that changes as the operating environment changes. Fine-tuning is almost always required, based on careful monitoring of results. In fact, adjustment is a continuing process—and will be until you implement a new plan. (Just remember that making adjustments is not the same as perpetually starting over, or operating ad hoc, or not really having a plan at all.)

Be ready to tweak, and to communicate to your people why you are making the changes. For example, competitors take actions that force a response. Market conditions change. The economy turns down. Life happens—and plans must adapt.

Let's say we plan to sell phones at seventy-five dollars on average, and the competition announces a major price cut that takes their average price down to fifty dollars. In the competitive wireless market, you typically need to match such a move. What does that mean? We must lower expenses somewhere else, or we sell a different kind of handset, or do both.

If a plan fails because the underlying assumptions changed, I don't view it as a failure so long as the plan was thoughtfully developed and implemented. My reaction is, okay, the plan isn't working. What are we going to do to make sure we still hit our targets?

A common question I am asked is, how soon do you adjust a plan? The answer is simple. Early. That is a key reason I believe in keeping a close eye on key metrics, something we will explore in depth in Chapter 12.

If I start to see numbers off target by 5 percent, I look for a reason. The explanation could be an unplanned event—wildfires in California, or snow storms on the East Coast. A seasoned manager usually will put me on alert that the event will cause a shortfall. In such a case, no adjustment is needed.

What I do worry about is when things go south 5 percent this month, another 3 to 4 percent the next, and I don't know why. I'll pick up the phone and ask what is going on. This allows me to test whether that particular manager really has a handle on his or her business. I do exactly the same thing when a program is going better than expected. I'll say, "Great results, What happened? What are you doing right here? What can we share with everyone else?"

Whether results are better or worse than plan, if the leader knows why, I feel confident about that individual. Conversely, I worry if someone doesn't know why results are above or below projections. Then I begin to think, *We need to watch you a little more carefully.* There are times when all adjustments in the world won't be enough. If conditions have changed dramatically, or if a key factor was misunderstood, the only course may be to redo the plan. Making this call takes experience. You learn over time how to judge whether to tweak or revamp. This is why the Learning Cycle we talked about in Chapter 4 is so important.

Markers on Your Personal Plan

If you reach a certain point in life and you say, "I haven't accomplished everything I wanted to do," the odds are you didn't adjust your personal plan along the way. Even with plenty of warning, we don't always pay attention.

Assuming you have a clear view of your desired destination, there are almost always some very clear markers that tell you whether you are on the right path. If you want to be a doctor, you know there are certain courses you will have to take, and you know you're going to have to do an internship. If you want to be a consultant, you know your first few years will involve a lot of airplane and hotel time. Either you do what your goal requires, or you choose a new goal. There's no middle ground.

A personal plan can be a lot less detailed than a business plan, but the framework of major elements (like obtaining the resources of time and money) is just as critical. I haven't met many people, either personally or professionally, smart enough to get where they want to go by making it up as they go along.

Takeaway Messages

Hope is not a strategy. You need a detailed game plan, one that outlines what you want to accomplish. That plan should have these five parts:

1. A brutally honest **assessment** of the situation you face.

2. A crystal clear **vision** of what you want to achieve.

3. A concise **explanation** of how you will achieve the vision. (Hint: You may want to be more ambitious than you originally thought. Why make incremental progress when you can do something significant?)

4. A solid **alignment** of the right people and the necessary resources to execute the plan. This is key to bringing your plan to fruition.

5. Room for **adjustment.** Life is not predictable. No matter how much preparation you do, you will need to alter your plan. That's just life. Accept it—and use it to your advantage.

NINE

Transforming Vision into Results

One of the best-selling business books of recent times had a simple and powerful title. *Execution* by Larry Bossidy, the former chairman and CEO of Honeywell, and Ram Charan, one of the most sought-after business consultants, made the point that generating ideas is simple. If you had to, you could probably come up with a dozen ideas for a new product or service before lunch. The key, they said correctly, was turning those ideas into reality. To be successful, you need to come up with new ideas *and* execute them effectively.

What follows from that holds true whether we are talking about business or life. Creating a vision is not enough. You also need to construct a plan that will turn that vision into a reality, a plan that assigns roles and responsibilities for making it happen.

As we saw in the previous chapter, a good plan identifies

- the top priorities,

- the key progress indicators you need to hit along the way to make sure you remain on course during your journey, and

- who is responsible for making what happen.

Each element of the plan is a critical ingredient in your recipe for success. Most people understand this intuitively. And most of us are pretty good at identifying the top priorities and the benchmarks we need to hit along the way. Failure often relates to the third element: who is responsible for what.

Do It or Fail

Assigning responsibility and accountability has three critical steps:

- First, decide who is in charge of what.
- Second, clearly communicate roles and responsibilities to those you want to tap.
- Third, be just as clear in communicating those roles and responsibilities to the rest of the organization.

A breakdown at any point means either chaos or inertia.

This is not a very hard concept, but in action it can be challenging. It takes discipline to tell people, "This is how it's going to be," and more discipline to hold them accountable.

When I work with people, I make sure everyone understands that we are going to have a clear strategy, a clear game plan, and clear accountability. There will be no confusion about who does what job, and no gaps left because of unassigned responsibilities.

In my experience, the best way to accomplish clarity, accountability, and focus is through a concise and well-documented plan summary. It spells out vision, strategies/initiatives, goals, and key metrics, or measurements for success. People can see what is expected of them. This avoids uncertainty and misalignment, and their inevitable companion, disappointing results.

Never Say, "No Way"

I'm one of those people who believes if the goal is important enough, there is always a solution for reaching it. In extremely unusual situations, careful planning doesn't always deliver results, but that doesn't mean there is no way. It just means it's time to take an unorthodox approach.

A couple of days after Hurricane Andrew, as we were fighting around the clock to maintain the network on backup generators, one of our key tandem switching centers started to have problems. The generator was overheating and wasn't going to last long. It was essential to get commercial power back on in the area—otherwise, we would lose the capability of switching calls throughout South Florida. Following our emergency-management guide, we tried repeatedly to contact the power company supervisor responsible for the area. But he wasn't responding to our calls or pages.

We tried escalating up the chain of command at the power company, but in the chaos of the moment, none of our contingency plans were working. There was one last thing to try. I called the supervisor's home, even though I knew he was out somewhere working. His wife answered. After telling her who I was and how serious our network problem was about to become, I asked her, "Do you get along with your husband?" She hesitated, then laughed and said, "Yes, I think so." I asked her if she would try paging her husband to phone home and then explain to him our desperate need to get power restored for the tandem switching center. It worked. We were running on commercial power within a couple of hours. The network stayed up.

Common Mistakes

Except for events like category 5 hurricanes (the most severe), thorough planning normally provides the answers a situation needs. But there are some common pitfalls that are made in planning.

One such pitfall is unrealistic goals—either too easy or too ambitious. If the economy is booming and you make a lowball growth projection for a hot product, I'm likely to say, "We can hit that target without a plan. What are you adding?"

Conversely, aiming for a doubling of year-over-year sales is going to require a higher power than you or I can control. Unless circumstances are truly extraordinary, it won't happen.

So, you need realistic goals, but goals that challenge and stretch you and members of your organization to perform at their very best. Let's assume that a 5 percent increase in revenues should be relatively simple for a mature business—that's not a goal that will inspire your team. Growth of 10 percent would require more effort, but it's been done before, and it could be done again. So let's put the revenue goal at a 15 percent increase. That's a stretch goal worth pursuing.

Now, how are you going to achieve it? What's the plan? Who is responsible for doing what? Spelling it all out is critical for several reasons.

First, any journey needs a road map, or you wind up in the weeds. "We'll figure it out as we go" is a sure-fire formula for failure. Conversely, if you make responsibilities clear, people will believe the plan is doable. They will execute well when they know what they must do, when they need to do it, and why it matters to the overall mission.

Second, a stretch goal without a clear plan will tempt people to take shortcuts, as we covered in the earlier discussion about ethical behavior. Take this route and you are asking for trouble.

Third, your own credibility as a leader is at stake. It will suffer if you give people big goals and poor direction for reaching for them.

I put a lot of responsibility on both the person who creates the plan to lay out exactly what needs to be done, and on those charged with carrying out the assignments that make up the plan.

If all this sounds obvious, I can tell you that even the most experienced executives sometimes forget to do it. They put down a number—we are going to increase sales by X, or profits by Y—and that's it. Just as hope is not a strategy, setting a target is not a plan.

In the previous chapter I explained how we created the vision, strategies, and tactics for BellSouth Latin America. The graphic that follows lays out the key elements of the plan.

BellSouth Latin America Operating Plan Elements

This type of clarity about the vision, strategies, tactics, and values is critical for the people responsible for the plan's execution. A clear, concise operating plan unifies an organization, assigns accountability, and enables great execution.

Now let's fast-forward to my experience at Cingular Wireless and look at the key elements of its operating plan. Notice the similarity to the BellSouth Latin America operating plan. This comparison highlights that the same elements work in domestic and international settings.

If you lay out your top priorities, identify what you need to get there, and clearly identify who is responsible for getting things done, you will be successful. And that is whether you are talking about business or your personal life.

Cingular Wireless Operating Plan Elements

What Will It Take to Reach Your Personal Goal?

You need to have a plan in your personal life as well. Most people can figure out the first piece, their goal, without too much difficulty. And they intuitively understand the third piece, that they are the person for making it happen. But the second piece, identifying what it will take to get there, is the place where many personal plans fail.

When I talk to people about their goals—what they want to

accomplish—I often hear things like, "I want to be a CEO, but I would rather not spend a lot of time in operations." Either they don't understand the value that certain types of experience add to their development, or they aren't willing to put in the hard work to make their dream happen. Regardless of which reason applies, their plan is flawed.

A closely related barrier that I see very often is impatience. Young people want success to come very quickly. It is hard to convince many of them that every step in a career-development path matters. Frontline experience, in particular, provides the best window on how an organization really works. Yes, it will take a little time. But once you've absorbed the lessons, the sky is the limit!

Personal development means paying the price to learn, not just to check off a line of boxes. Moving too fast, shortchanging the learning cycle, and failing to absorb the invaluable lessons of experience have derailed far more promising careers than they have enhanced.

One last point: if you find yourself dreading or avoiding an experience that you know is vital to your goal, maybe it's time to rethink the goal itself.

As Stan Sigman, former CEO of AT&T Mobility, would often say, a good plan is a job half done. You need to develop the plan, align the people and resources needed to execute it, and communicate what needs to be done. So we turn to the topic of communication in the next chapter.

Takeaway Messages

Executing ideas is the most difficult thing to do.
Coming up with ideas is (relatively) easy. Turning
those ideas into reality is (extremely) difficult.

How will you get there? Once you develop a vision,
you need a plan to carry it out. You also need to
assign accountability. Otherwise nothing gets done.

If the task is to be accomplished, everyone needs
to (a) understand the overall plan, (b) know his or her
specific role and how to do it, and (c) be held
accountable.

A game plan for your life is developed in the same
manner as a game plan for business. The only
difference is you are the only person responsible for
carrying it out!

TEN

Communicate, Communicate, Communicate!

One day, when I was responsible for the BellSouth network in several states, I rode with a repair technician in Florida. As we headed out in the morning, I could tell he was a little nervous—not unusual under the circumstances. Finally he said what was on his mind: "Do you want me to do this the way I would do it if you weren't here?"

It was an insightful question. What he really was asking, in a nice way, was whether I was there for show, or to really learn.

Most definitely the answer was to learn! I believe the most valuable time a leader in our company spends is with frontline employees, observing them doing the basic work of our business. Keeping the network running. Handling customer calls in a call center. Interacting with customers in our stores.

Communicating with frontline employees on the job teaches me things no spreadsheet or weekly report could ever reveal.

Also, just being there communicates something to them that is extremely important. It tells employees that the leadership of the company understands the importance of their role and wants to support them to the maximum degree.

While we were rebuilding the network in the aftermath of Hurricane Andrew, I was riding with a technician and we wound up at a distribution point, which is a local node for cross-connecting facilities. Another technician arrived who also needed to perform a task at the same distribution point. He didn't really notice me because I always dress for field work on these ride-alongs. Almost immediately the second tech started complaining about how management was not being responsive to some of their issues. I can still see my ride-along technician making faces and gesturing, trying to signal to his friend. But I was glad to hear it. I stepped up and told the unhappy tech who I was, and that I was there for the very reason he said, to learn what they needed to get this job done. He was impressed to the point that he went back and told everybody at the work center that de la Vega was in the field, riding with technicians and listening to the issues they faced! The impact was almost as strong as if I had ridden with them individually.

In Latin America, where the work culture tends to be very hier-archical, I took special measures to reach out to our people. We scheduled a "Talk to Ralph" day when any employee could call a special number and tell me their ideas about the business. There were so many calls, our lines were jammed. These employees responded to the sheer novelty of the boss asking what was on their minds. In one office, a group assembled in the break room so they could pass the phone around. I admired their ingenuity, but after conversing with a couple of them, I had to move on to take calls from other countries.

As you can see, the heart of my communication philosophy is to get out from behind the desk, either physically or virtually, and into the real world of frontline employees serving customers. A leader can give great speeches and write inspiring memos, but power that comes from communication starts with being an open-minded listener and learner.

From that core, you build outward using all the many tools that modern technology puts at your disposal. Let's dive deeper into what makes a leader an effective communicator.

"Walk This Way"

If you have seen the movie *Young Frankenstein,* you recognize the header above as a line from the film. Without recounting the scene, let me just note that there is more than one way to interpret "walk this way." Unfortunately, ambiguous communication is not always as humorous as that moment in the movie.

What could be easier than communicating with those under your leadership? You want to get a particular thing done, and you tell the people you supervise. You give them guidelines for how to do the task. Then you sit back and wait for the successful completion. Why doesn't it happen just like you said?

The reality, as we all know, is that getting things done is harder than most of us could ever imagine. A key reason is that we don't communicate effectively, and this chapter examines why. In the process, I will describe some of the communications tools that I advocate. As you will see later in the chapter. I believe that being clear, concise, and consistent—what I call the three Cs—provides the key to communicating well.

More than Once

No matter how many times you communicate a message, it's never enough. This can be a hard concept for some managers—especially new managers—to grasp and understand. They assume that because they are in charge, people are hanging on their every word. It doesn't work like that.

We live in the midst of distractions, and nowhere more than on the job.

I'm listening to you while looking at my BlackBerry, so I miss a single word that changes everything. Or I am thinking about a deadline I have coming up, or worrying about the four e-mails in my in-box marked urgent. Or I just got a text message from one of my kids who has a problem. I want to pay attention to you; I intend to pay attention. But then life intervenes. It's a rare conversation that doesn't include some form of interruption or momentary loss of attention.

So the first rule of delivering a message is to repeat it, and then repeat it again. Sure, you'll use different methods (more on this later), but the bottom line is, *repeat, reiterate, reemphasize.* One telling will not make it sink in.

Why do you see the same TV commercial a number of times? Because repetition makes it more effective. Advertisers know that without multiple impressions, the commercial doesn't sink in. Why would it be any different in talking to employees? They are your customers in a sense, so you should expect to have to repeat what you say in order to get through to them. Communicating clearly is just good customer service.

Another, more subtle reason that you don't get through is that an emphasis on timely communication may not be built into your company's infrastructure. Let's say I decide to change a certain policy, and I make this known very clearly in a companywide memo, followed up by a speech. But one out of ten employees is new each year. They weren't in the audience to hear my speech. They never saw the memo. The changed policy doesn't get updated in the employee procedures right away. If a situation comes up related to the policy, confusion will reign.

To make sure all our salespeople hear the same thing in the same way, we established a special Saturday morning procedure in our AT&T Mobility stores. Before opening, we set aside some time to go over procedural changes, new promotions, new products, and other timely topics. Before we started these "huddles," maybe an employee would read the memo or maybe not. If he was new, he might read the memo but not really get it. If she was a veteran, maybe she didn't read carefully enough to notice a point-of-sale change and kept ringing up something in the old way. Now, in just a few minutes, everyone is brought up to speed: just in time for our busiest sales day of the week. This process brings me back to the 3 Cs of effective communication.

3 Cs of Communications

Clear   Concise   Consistent

Clear

The first rule of great communications is to make sure you communicate a very clear message. Great communicators take complex subjects and make them very simple and easy to understand. When making speeches or giving informal talks, I always like to begin by telling my listeners what I'm going to tell them; then I tell them; and finally I close by summarizing and telling them again. I have found this format forces me to be very clear about the message I am trying to communicate.

Concise

The second rule is you have to be concise and to the point. Whether it's an e-mail, a memo, or a speech, my advice is the same: Make it short, sweet, and focused. If what you say is overly complex, you've got a badly crafted message.

Mark Twain once apologized to a friend for writing a long letter, explaining that he didn't have time to write a short one. The thought remains valid more than a hundred years later. Brief, effective communication takes real effort, with every word and image carefully chosen for impact. Compared to Twain's time, attention spans of the twenty-first century are short and getting shorter. A well-honed, effective message makes its point without superfluous clutter.

Consistent

The third rule is you have to be consistent with your message. Changing messages from week to week or month to month leads to confusion and impairs communications.

As you have seen, I love getting out among our people and talking about what we need to do. To me, nothing is more important than communicating with our employees. I love encouraging them, explaining our goals, clarifying why we're doing things a certain way, and letting them know what I need them to do to make AT&T Mobility the company we all want it to be. This is the fun, energizing part of the job.

After ten essentially similar presentations over two weeks or so, they can start to feel redundant. But I realize that for my audience, even if they've heard the key points before, the repetition is reassuring instead of redundant. They are getting a steady, consistent message that builds confidence. It is a strong confirmation that the organization is on the right track and pressing forward.

I tell people who complain about making too many presentations that if they skimp on consistent communication, they will be less effective as leaders. The message won't get through, and the result will be frustration and disappointing outcomes. In addition, I remind them that leaders are always communicating, whether they realize it or not. The absence of communication carries its own message. Personally, I would much rather craft and shape the communication instead of leaving a vacuum that could be filled by misinformation and rumor.

Provide Context to Aid Understanding

Explaining *why* is always part of any effective communication. "Do this" is not a very persuasive message. The more people understand the reason behind a strategy, an initiative, or a change of plan, the better chance it has of accomplishing what you intended.

After all, as a leader you want your audience to become secondary communicators on your behalf, carrying your message to others in the organization. Providing context helps them be effective in this role—especially managers who are responsible for spreading the word to their own teams. The more they understand, the more credible they will be as spokespersons.

In addition, if an employee understands *why* a particular course of action is being taken, it affects his or her approach on the job. You can't anticipate what frontline people will face as they interact with customers. The more *why* they have, the more likely they are to represent the company in exactly the way you hope.

For this same reason, it's important to link communication back to the company's fundamental vision, mission, and strategies. Doing this provides "context for the context" and conveys the organic connection among what is being done, why, and what it all means. Employees who are accustomed to receiving this type of strategic communication will know how to react even if a specific situation has never come up before. They will know the kinds of actions and behavior that are expected.

Tailoring the Message

One size does not fit all in communicating. Every employee in a company contributes to achieving the vision and fulfilling the strategies in different ways. Making a personal connection can be powerfully motivating. Obviously you don't discuss return on invested capital (ROIC) the same way to customer service reps as you would to the company's financial specialists. But you *do* talk about it—by connecting the calls they handle, the sales they make, the business they preserve, to ROIC. If you're reviewing overall company performance for one department, you need to make the link between departmental metrics and the organization as a whole. If leadership of your industry is part of the company vision, this involves very specific achievements for a team of network technicians versus different achievements for a retail sales force. It's important to translate the concept of leadership from abstract to concrete.

And always remember this: one of the biggest mistakes a leader can make is to speak over people's heads. On the other hand, never leave them feeling as if you talked down to them or wasted their time.

Delivery Formats

I've worked in the communications business all my adult life, and it amazes me to realize how the ways to communicate have exploded through the years. Today a leader can reach out with a text message, a podcast, a webcast, an e-mail, or a video e-mail. They all have a place.

But for my money, the most effective is still the face-to-face personal talk. Seeing how people react is invaluable. Nothing gives you the feel of your employees' attitudes and the mood of the moment like being in front of them.

I'm an advocate of using a variety of delivery techniques, depending on the subject or just to keep things fresh. I might do a speech with no visuals, for example. But different people learn in different ways, so the next time I'll support the speech with heavy visuals, from slides to video clips. For some subjects, numbers and graphs work well (but not too many—nothing makes the air go out of a room like a data-heavy slide show).

The ultimate objective is the same, no matter how you deliver it: get your message across in a way that lets it be understood and believed. This means making it easy for people to receive what you say. I learned this the hard way. As I've already mentioned, early in my career I was a terrible public speaker. After working hard at my delivery and learning how to be comfortable in front of a group, I still had a serious flaw—diving into too much detail. The audience would get lost, especially when I used all the slang and acronyms that are so much a part of telecoms lingo. Probably not one in ten people in the room really followed what I was saying.

In time I realized the power of personal translation—telling people what the information means for *them*. Today, when I'm presenting a complex topic, I work hard to make it simple without losing the sense of importance. I've learned to put myself in the audience's shoes and ask, "What do I need to know?" And that's what I seek to deliver. Of the many miles I've progressed in my career, improvement as a communicator is one of the most significant advancements. I wouldn't be here otherwise.

Feedback Loop

As an engineer, I've always known it takes two things to communicate: a transmitter and a receiver.

Some managers think communication is just about the transmitting part. They believe if you have put the message out there, communication is accomplished. I prefer the adage "God gave you two ears and one mouth. So listen twice as much as you talk."

This is why we do feedback surveys after any major talk I give. We ask questions such as: Was the message clear? Do you understand how it affects you? Was your time well spent? There are several reasons for this follow-up: to confirm the message got through, and also to monitor any action that is being taken as a result. It's one thing for a call-center employee to hear me say that the goal is for calls to be answered within twenty seconds. It is quite another thing to go back to the cubicle and do it.

Another reason for following up is to detect if people have misunderstood. I find it amazing that even the most straightforward statements can be misunderstood. If you make a statement to a group of ten people, at least one of them will hear it wrong. Without the feedback system, you might not discover the misunderstanding until it has had bad consequences.

As a communicator, part of my job is to send a message asking you to do the things we need to do. The other part is to coach you to make sure it gets done. That's why the feedback loop is crucial.

Authenticity

When you are communicating to employees, make sure you are yourself, first and foremost. Of course you are speaking for the company, yet the impact will be much stronger if you are your authentic self.

Find a way to make a personal connection. For me, the best way is to shake the hand of each person as he or she enters the room. This greeting communicates that I'm not just there to spout the company line. I'm Ralph de la Vega, a human being talking to human beings. People are more willing to listen, and to give you honest feedback, if you impress them as a real person, approachable, and interested in them.

On some days I've shaken as many as one thousand hands (and yes, my hand hurt that night). Long ago I lost count of how many people told me, "No executive has ever come down here and shaken my hand."

Just as important, I always leave time for dialogue after I speak. Some executives don't like unscripted, unrehearsed interaction because they're uncomfortable with the possibility of not having all the answers. Sometimes I don't have the answers either, and I say so. What matters is that I come away from the Q&A knowing a lot more about what people are thinking and feeling. When I don't have an answer, I make a point to find it out and get back to whoever asked the question.

Maybe you won't be comfortable with this style at first. But try it out, and I bet you come to see its value.

Let me give you an example that comes from a company we acquired in the past. It had a very strong command structure. Orders came from headquarters, and the job of field forces was to implement without questioning. You were punished if you were perceived to step out of line. In such an environment, people won't question a decision even if they know it's wrong.

That culture came back to haunt them when they rolled out a new technology. Headquarters ordered a change that left gaps in the customers' cell phone coverage. The network engineers had known all along this would happen, but on account of the rigid culture, they did not raise the issue with headquarters. A little two-way communication would have avoided some seriously unhappy customers.

Personal Communication

What message do you want to send about yourself?

I had to face that question early in my career. I had started on the network side of our company, and I got comfortable communicating in a very direct manner to the field operations personnel. Then they moved me to sales. And the first time I talked to a large number of employees in a call center, I made some of them very upset. I didn't think I had been that tough, but apparently I came across that way to them.

My first reaction was, "What's wrong with these people? None of the network folks I ever worked with got upset with how I talked to them." And then I realized that the problem wasn't them. It was me. You can't take the same approach with everyone.

I was trying to communicate that the call center needed to improve sales performance, which indeed was the case. But I was too blunt, and it came across as insensitive. Today, if I were to deliver the same information, I would frame the message very differently.

Through every action you take—how you talk, dress, stand, and write—you are communicating something about yourself. What message do you want to send about you and your personal brand? Is that the message that others are receiving?

How can you tell? Well, you can ask people. And you can pay attention to how people react to you. (You can always get a sense if you pay attention.) Even if the feedback isn't favorable, you will learn and grow by seeking it out and accepting what it tells you.

If the organization's performance is falling short of what you expect, it's very likely that communication is part of the problem. Make sure that your message is crystal clear and well understood. Not only will results improve, but so will your own personal brand as a leader.

Takeaway Messages

Communicate, communicate, communicate. You can never do it enough.

Listening and learning are the critical starting points.

Remember the 3 Cs: Your communication must be clear, concise, and consistent.

Establish a feedback loop to make sure your message has gotten through efficiently. No matter what form, every communication has two components: transmission and reception. You want to make sure your message has been received.

Be authentic, and remember that everything about you communicates!

ELEVEN

Maximizing People's Potential

At Cingular, we used to have a rule that said if a customer called to complain about a legitimate charge on his or her bill, the customer service rep could reduce the charge by 50 percent.

Of course, if we had made a mistake, we would give you a 100 percent refund. But these situations were different. Often they involved customers running up charges unaware. For example, they added text messaging to their accounts and they—or more likely their children—went way over the limit on the messages included in the plan, so they were being charged for each additional message.

When something like this happened, our old rule was: listen to the customer; explain what happened ("These are text message charges, and there were a lot of them, as you can see"); and then offer to reduce the charge by half if the customer was unaware of what was included in the plan. If there was a hundred-dollar charge, we would take fifty dollars off the bill.

151

It was a very simple rule. But it did not enable or empower the employee to solve the customer's problem. All it did was provide a robotic response, in essence handcuffing the rep. The customer would say, "Gosh, I didn't know you charged so much for text messaging" [or whatever], and all the rep could say was, "I can take 50 percent off; that's it."

One end result was unhappy customers who thought they were being penalized unfairly for not understanding their plan. The other end result was frustrated reps that couldn't do their main job of helping customers. Not an optimal customer service scenario.

So we decided to enable and empower the reps. In this case, empowerment meant giving them the tools to solve the problem in a customer-centric way. If a customer complained about a hundred dollars in text-messaging charges, the rep had the authority to say, "I can see that is the first time this happened. And if you had our unlimited text messaging plan for twenty dollars a month, you wouldn't have had this problem. I can add this plan for you right now and make it retroactive to last month, so all you owe us is twenty dollars. Would you like for me to do that?"

Bam! Problem solved.

We enabled the rep to address the situation—no more robotic response. And at the same time we told them, in effect, "We know you are capable of solving customer problems. We have confidence in your judgment. We are going to trust you to make the customer happy and generate some revenue for us—the twenty dollars a month going forward, as you feel the situation warrants." This approach has worked out beautifully.

There is an old saying I like a lot: When you hire someone's hands, you get his brain for free.

The point: If you let them, employees are capable of doing much more than the specific task for which they have been hired. Allowing them to use their full potential is empowerment. You want to enable the people who work for you to do as much as they possibly can within the framework you establish.

The *How* of Empowerment

We wanted to put our reps in a position to make the right decision but not run the risk of giving the store away. So we analyzed the situations they were encountering most frequently—the ten things customers called about most often. No surprise, the most frequent call went something like this: "I gave my son this plan that included two hundred text messages a month, and I thought there was no way he could possibly send more. But he did."

For other most-frequent problems, we found other ways to empower our reps. Results have been extraordinary, evident in improved customer satisfaction and employee satisfaction scores.

In any business, a big part of successful empowerment is establishing good boundaries and limits. For example, if one of your employees is assisting a longstanding, loyal customer, there is more leeway than for one with a bad credit history. But it boils down to this: your team members want to help customers. They get crossed up when a company policy prevents them from providing what they think is quality service, which also happens to be the kind of service you want them to provide.

Empower Senior Staff Too

Our management structure is designed to empower up and down the organization. When we merged AT&T Wireless with Cingular to form the largest wireless company in the U.S., we divided the combined company into twenty-seven different geographic segments. Each segment was assigned a vice president/general manager (VP/GM) who was given profit-and-loss (P&L) responsibility for the territory, plus the latitude that such accountability requires. The VP/GM could change the pricing of handsets, modify ads for their market, hire and fire. In short, they were given the power to run the business. This has remained our model at AT&T Mobility because it is highly effective. Our people know they are empowered, and they aren't afraid to pull the levers. In addition, as a company we stay closer to customers than centralized control would allow.

The move paid off. Over the most recent three-year time period, we grew margin percentages from the mid-20s to the low 40s while adding more than twenty million customers.

Among those twenty-seven VP/GM positions, their territories range from a large and established market like New York to a relatively small but fast-growing market like Arizona/New Mexico. This provides a career track for senior managers, since you don't want to put a first-time VP/GM in charge of huge markets like New York, Los Angeles, or Chicago. The structure provides a very logical progression and succession path. The individual who runs Southern California (Los Angeles) previously ran South Texas.

Our Northern California (our largest market) VP/GM previously ran Chicago and prior to that Oklahoma and Arkansas. By the time they took over the larger markets, they were ready to be superstars.

The more you empower your people, the more ownership they take. The tough thing is to give them enough control to be successful while staying within the company's bounds of acceptable risk.

As the company's leader, ultimate responsibility falls on me. That's why I would never put somebody in New York who hadn't proven him- or herself in a smaller job. In a small market, you can take that risk. If a new person goes in and makes a terrible mistake and we have a bad month or bad quarter, we can live with it as an investment in growing a new generation of leadership. But I can't afford a terrible mistake in New York. The market is just too big.

Successful empowerment requires that the person is ready to accept empowerment. You can pay a huge price by promoting someone who is not ready and lacks the experience and seasoning to make good decisions. I discussed this earlier in the "Learn to Unlearn and Relearn" chapter.

Starting in a smaller market, a new VP/GM is not treated any differently than those in large markets. Everyone is held to exactly the same standards. Our model says that if the small market is well run, the individual probably will perform well in a bigger market too. On the other hand, those who don't work out in their initial VP/GM role are usually experiencing their first full P&L job, which simply isn't for everyone. Better to learn this sooner rather than later.

We have markets segmented into three categories: A, B, and C markets, C being the smallest. And typically a VP/GM advances from a C to a B market, and then from a B to an A. The beauty of this concept is the ability to test people. A manager might have an MBA from a great graduate school, might have held high-level staff jobs, and may perform extremely well at meetings. But until you put that person on the front lines and he or she experiences the real world, you cannot know for sure.

That's why, when we do career planning and identify candidates for the next big promotion, I give first consideration to those who have delivered in the past, as opposed to someone with a great résumé who has been to the right schools and fits in with the group. If you have been on the line multiple times and delivered, you are going to be at the top of my list. You have proven you can do the job.

Feedback and Accountability

Empowerment works in tandem with accountability. This means providing managers with metrics that give real-time feedback on progress being made against goals. At AT&T Mobility, we use a simple set of metrics called the "Four Rs" to give us this feedback. This works whether you run a billion-dollar company or an ice cream shop or an ad agency.

The 4 R's

Rate of
Penetration
(R1)

Revenue
Intensity
(R2)

Return on
Operations
(R3)

Reputation
(R4)

- The first one is *Rate of Penetration.* How many customers do you have out of the population you serve? The New York market might have ten million wireless customers in all. How many of them are yours?

- The second metric is *Revenue Intensity.* We are looking at how much you are selling to the customers you already have. How much revenue are those customers generating? Are you selling them all the products you should?

- Next is *Return on Operations.* How profitable are you? Are margins increasing?

- And the last piece is *Reputation,* or customer loyalty. You've got a lot of customers; but are you retaining them?

Empowerment cuts both ways. A VP/GM may say, "I need $2 million more to do X." And my answer might be, "Well, what are you doing with the other $20 million you've got? This is your sandbox. We're given you a $20 million operating budget, and you can basically move it around the way you want. Why aren't you shifting some of that money to obtain the $2 million you need?"

But let's say you are using that $20 million as efficiently as possible and are maxed out. If this is the case, you will need to show me the additional revenue and profits that will be generated by the additional $2 million investment, and be willing to commit to these improvements as part of your plan. The investment you are proposing will then be compared to other options that compete for the company's capital.

But my first question always will be, "Why can't you handle what you want to do with the money you have today? After all, this is why we empowered you."

I use a similar accountability approach when visiting in the field. Inevitably somebody will say, "In our local market we have this issue; what do you recommend we do?" My response typically is, "Time-out. Ask your VP/GM." I will recognize that VP/GM in the audience and make the point that he or she is the local leader who makes the call. And then we measure the results of those calls as a gauge of the leader's good judgment.

For instance, let's say the VP/GM makes a convincing case to expand our retail presence in a particular market. We will commit the funds after reviewing the business case, but the VP/GM recommends what is the best approach for the market: opening a new store, relocating an existing store, or doing a renovation. The VP/GM knows the market and is in the best position to decide which strategy will generate the best return on investment.

Just as the company empowers top managers, we expect them to empower others. Part of a VP/GM's role is to enable a store manager to run an optimal operation, including giving him the authority to make an unhappy customer happy again.

Empowerment goes down the line. We challenge our store managers to rethink how they do business. They are not just confined to the walls of the store. We want them thinking outside the box, literally. It's not just about walk-in customers. There's a small business across the street, or a condominium complex down the road, where you could be selling. The job is to get business, with the store as a vehicle but not a fence.

Maybe there's a small business nearby that could boost productivity if the staff had BlackBerry devices. Or you could work with the local Small Business team to set up a demo of the iPhone before the store opens for local businesses. This is entrepreneurship, which we strongly encourage; we like to spread the successes.

Personal Empowerment

How do you empower yourself? I think the question really is, how do you keep from disempowering yourself? How do you make the choice *not* to impose self-limitations by thinking, *I can't do this. I can't do that*? Why not make the choice to be the very best at what you want to do?

So ask yourself, "If I did X, Y, and Z, could I be the best?" And if you believe the answer is yes, ask yourself why you are not doing these things. Why disempower yourself?

Some people are quick to say, "I am a victim of this or a victim of that." Giving in to a victim mentality means you've lost control of your journey. The victim has taken the wheel, and it won't be a pleasant ride.

The world is full of choices and opportunities for you. Take them.

Takeaway Messages

To get the most out of people, enable and empower them. Give them the right tools and sufficient authority to make decisions that will allow them to take care of customers and grow the business.

Empower at all levels. Everyone can be empowered. Clearly, you don't give someone who has joined you right out of high school or college multimillion-dollar responsibilities. But no matter where they are on the organization chart, people can be empowered.

Think about this strategically. Regularly, and often, check on how well people are handling their responsibilities. You want to know if they doing well so you can give them even more authority. And you also need to know if there is a problem so you can correct it as soon as possible. (Yes, you want to empower them, but you are still ultimately responsible.)

No personal boundaries. Don't let anyone— especially you—put a limit on what you can accomplish.

TWELVE

You Get What You Measure— and Then Some

Even people who have never heard of Peter Drucker, perhaps the most influential management thinker who ever lived, have heard his maxim: What gets measured gets done. And like just about everything Dr. Drucker said about accomplishing objectives, this one is absolutely right.

When most people first hear "what gets measured gets done," they say, "I get it. If I know my boss is watching how much progress I am making toward something she has asked me to do, then for sure I am going to work on it."

And that is absolutely right. Measurements are milestones that help you understand whether you're advancing toward your goals. But if you stop there in your interpretation of Dr. Drucker's statement, you only get partial credit. The power of measurements is much bigger.

If you think about what we have talked about so far in this book, you will see how this all comes together. To achieve your vision, you need to utilize the right strategies and create the right initiatives. Then you need the right metrics—you need to measure the right things—to monitor your progress and stay on course. Graphically it looks like the triangle below.

When it comes to metrics, three things matter:

1. Choosing the right ones.

2. Tracking performance against those metrics.

3. Displaying progress so that (a) everyone knows how they are doing toward achieving the goals, and (b) it is easy to spot areas needing improvement.

I believe that measurements should be visible and color coded. Red means there is work to be done; yellow indicates we may need to pay attention to this; and green shows we are in good shape.

Choose the Right Metrics

What should you measure? In theory you could measure literally thousands of factors—everything from employee-retention rates to return on assets, from customer satisfaction to sales growth over time, from how fast you are progressing in your career to how quickly your bank account is growing, and display all those things in prominent places to show that they are important.

But if *everything* is important, then nothing is. Measuring is a way of focusing the organization's energy and effort.

I learned in my first operational job that you couldn't chase forty different measurements. You had to make it clear to employees which were the important measures so they would not be overwhelmed. No one can deal with directives such as "Goals 1 through 10 are important today, goals 12 through 27 are important tomorrow, and next week we are only going to concentrate on goals 22 through 28."

If you tell people what you want them to do, most people will try to do it. But if you change objectives every week, you end up chasing your tail because there are too many things to track and measure.

And if you go the other way and just lay out dozens upon dozens of things you think are important but never rank them, then people will prioritize on their own. Their objectives and yours may not be the same.

That's why you want a handful of measures—four or five at the absolute most—for people to concentrate on. The key is to find out which ones make the most difference, and focus on them.

Focus on the factors that will have the biggest impact on achieving your goals—the things that, if you do them well, will give you an 80 to 90 percent chance of success.

Based on my experience over the years, the right metrics need to pass the following three tests:

1. They need to be comparable across territories, geographies, product lines, and departments, if possible. While the actual results will differ, the metric should be the same both to focus the organization and benchmark performance.

2. They must present a balanced view of the goals of the business. A great example might be a pair of metrics, such as grow revenues and expand margins. Having both in play removes the incentive to blow away the revenue goals by selling low-margin products. It also reinforces the culture of winning the right way, as we previously discussed.

3. They should be quantifiable with accuracy, consistency, and frequency so that you can analyze progress and detect small deviations quickly. The right metrics will allow you to make adjustments while a problem is

small. It is critical that people believe the metrics are accurate and reflect true performance. Metrics should build trust and credibility, never undermine them.

Earlier when we discussed feedback and accountability, I presented the 4R model as the key metrics we used at AT&T Mobility to track progress against goals.

The 4 R's

Rate of Penetration (R1)

Revenue Intensity (R2)

Return on Operations (R3)

Reputation (R4)

How do the 4 Rs stack up against the tests I described above?

1. Are they comparable across the portfolio? Yes, absolutely. They are relevant in California or Georgia. Recall that R1 is Rate of Penetration, meaning how many customers you have out of the population you serve. California has a target, and Georgia has its own target. R1 applies to both because it's a rate, not a specific number of customers. On Revenue Intensity, R2, we're measuring the average revenue per customer. A large market will have more total revenue than a small

market, but on a per-customer basis, both can compete to deliver the best results.

2. Do they offer a balanced view of the company's goals? Yes. The 4 Rs provide great balance among customer growth, revenue growth, profitability, and customer loyalty.

3. Can they be measured with accuracy, frequency, and reliability? Again, the answer is yes. Each team can monitor its performance relative to a peer group, driving a healthy competitive culture.

Measuring

You tell me you want us to be number one in customer satisfaction? Terrific. How do we measure that? We want to be the employer of choice? Great. How do you define "employer of choice," and how will we know when we are there? In other words, what does victory look like?

You'd be surprised how often, when people are laying out a plan, they forget to include the metrics necessary to measure success. If you can't measure progress toward a goal, what's the use of having it? It's not a goal; it's a wish.

I challenge people on this all the time. "Okay, I heard your strategy. I understand what steps you want us to take. But how are we going to measure whether we are succeeding?" If this question can't be answered, the initiative has a high failure potential. So along with mastering the art of selecting the right metrics, you need to master the science of measuring them consistently, accurately, and reliably.

Color Coding

Colors are an easy visual cue that emphasize progress and status against a goal. I use the color code of a traffic light: red, yellow, and green. Red means our results are significantly below objectives, yellow indicates those that are slightly below where we want to be, and if we are in the green, then everything is fine. I like to see these measures in a prominent place, such as the center of the office, so everyone can know where we are at a given moment.

The beauty of charting your progress in this simple, easy-to-understand way is that you know at a glance whether you are on target. This is especially important if you are involved in a number of different initiatives simultaneously. You don't waste time wondering, *How are we doing?* You can tell instantly. You know where to focus attention—on the objectives that are colored red.

I have found this system is a great time-saver. It also has a very interesting psychological impact. If you are in charge of an initiative colored red, you are powerfully motivated to get that color changed! People don't like to see their names in red. They don't like to be associated with something that is failing. They will redouble their efforts to improve performance and results. But more important, they work hard so that red never touches their project in the first place.

This is the major reason why the progress report—the red, yellow, and green assessment—should be prominently displayed. If it is out in the open, in the spotlight, there is no way to hide poor performance. People are really motivated not to be in the red.

What kind of performance gets assigned to which category? Results that are 5 percent and 10 percent below objective should immediately be colored red. You want to know if something is going off trend early, rather than too late in the process. This amount of deviation early on calls for action.

In our use of the color code, the red-yellow-green results are not only publicly shared at headquarters; they are also distributed throughout the organization. Each region, every week, gets a red-yellow-green report on the key metrics. And if your region is in the red, everyone knows it. If you did not hit your sales this week, I am going to ask what happened. Was it just a holiday, or did you have a system outage? Is the economy in this part of the country going sour? What's going on?

If the region leadership answers, "We don't know," well, why don't you know? It's your business. If we set a bad target, okay, prove to me that we set a bad target. Is it something else? Let's figure it out. Today.

This system not only detects early problems; it puts pressure on the individuals to do their job and to think about the plan they create. If you pick numbers out of the air for your plan, this system will find you out very quickly.

Or, you could have created a great plan, but you haven't looked at it since you put it together, and now you are doing something completely different. It's time to figure out why you are not executing against what you created in the first place.

In summary, this approach builds discipline. It forces people to think about what they commit to do, then do what they say they're going to do.

Most people, if you ask them, would prefer not to have their numbers published, but that's not an option. If you are not all in the green, we will coach you and work with you to help you get there. For those who are constantly at the bottom even with coaching, the poor performance is a signal of the need for change.

We also used statistical process control charts where appropriate to track the variation of processes over time. The combination makes for a powerful fact-based metrics system.

Calling a Red on Yourself

This red-yellow-green approach also works well in helping you achieve the goals in your personal life. And it is easy to see why that is the case. Let's say that you want to be a doctor, an engineer, or a lawyer. Part of setting that goal is figuring out what you have to do to get there.

If your goal is to be a lawyer four years from now, then you should be doing certain things to get ready for that. Part of it is finishing your undergraduate degree if you haven't. Then you have to apply to a law school. You may want a clerkship. You should create a list of things you need to do, complete with deadlines, and you should track them with red, yellow, and green metrics.

The minute you begin to fall behind, you ought to call a red on yourself and say, "I said I was going to do this, and I didn't do it." Unless you do this, you will slide and say, "I'll do that tomorrow." And tomorrow may never come.

I can't tell you how many people come and talk to me and say, "I want to get ahead." And I say, "Okay. That's great. But you don't have a college degree. When are you going to get a college degree?"

"I'm going to start next month."

"Okay. Come talk to me then. Make an appointment as soon as you start."

Next month they don't make an appointment. And when I run into them later, I always ask, "Are you serious about this? Are you going to start? If you can't start next month, will you start next quarter? Do you have a commitment to start something that you told me was important to you?"

I know this is difficult. Odds are the individual has a full-time job. But people do it all the time. So, if you are not making progress toward the goal, you need to call a red on yourself and ask, "Am I serious about this? Do I need to find a different goal, or am I just going to always flounder?"

The system of red-yellow-green also works for long-term goals. Say you're a new engineer, and you want to be a senior manager in charge of engineers in ten years. You probably will start out as a field engineer. To accomplish your goal, your next job will probably have to be a staff assignment to learn how things are done in headquarters. Then you will go back out into the field in a supervisory capacity.

The point is, there's usually a progression of jobs you have to succeed at before you get to be a senior manager. If you don't follow that path, it won't happen. Even if someone likes you, even if you can talk a good game, even if you excel in meetings—and believe me, I've seen all those examples—you won't progress to your goal.

Those who succeed are constantly asking themselves, "What do I need to do in order to accomplish my goal?" and then they track their progress toward the desired destination.

Be honest with yourself, especially if you see a lot of reds as you chart your progress. Have you picked the right goals? Are you dedicated to them? If you're not achieving your goals, something is wrong, and you need an honest conversation with yourself. Is this what you really want to do? If not, find a different goal that inspires you to follow through.

Accountability is an inherent part of leadership, and measuring is fundamental to accountability. So if you aspire to lead, choosing and using metrics will be an important part of your future.

Takeaway Messages

Is it a goal or a wish? The objective you set is simply a wish, as in, "I wish I had ten million dollars," until you set out a specific plan for achieving it.

The plan should identify specific steps you need to take to achieve it. Figure out the four or five—usually no more than that—key objectives you need to reach in order to succeed. (If you set too many goals, you won't accomplish any.)

Constantly and relentlessly measure your progress on those key metrics. I've learned the best metrics pass three simple tests: (1) they are comparable across the organization, (2) they are balanced, and (3) they can be measured consistently, accurately, and reliably. The best way to track metrics and communicate progress is to use a color scheme. I use red, yellow, and green to easily identify results that are significantly below objective, slightly below objective, and at or above objective. This makes for a very powerful and effective visual.

THIRTEEN

Spotting Opportunities

Soon after I was assigned to a new operations job, I discovered we had an overloaded computer system that had reduced order processing to a crawl and was causing numerous delays. I learned the division had budgeted ten million dollars for an upgrade in the following year. This was fine, but we needed to address the problem right now. So I went to one of the most able and experienced people in the division and asked him to look into the problem and find an alternative. This excellent employee could not find a solution other than to spend the ten million dollars today—and that simply wasn't in our budget.

Then I asked the folks at headquarters to take a look, and they came up with the same answer. The person they assigned went out of his way to tell me the situation was hopeless. "Ralph, you are new here, so let me give you some advice," the person from headquarters said. "Everyone knows it is going to take ten million dollars to fix the problem. Just accept it."

Well, we didn't have ten million dollars. But we did have a huge problem. So I turned it over to one of the newest members of our team—a woman who, while young, knew a lot about computer systems. Fortunately for us, she did not have the same mental block as others. She was too green to know that this problem could not be solved. Her attitude was, *I was asked to find a solution, and that is exactly what I am going to do.*

Soon after looking into the problem, she had an idea. There were computers elsewhere in the company that were being underutilized and had excess capacity. We could share our load with them until we had the money for the upgrade. That's exactly what we did, and the stop-gap measure worked until we finally had the funds to upgrade the system. It took a new employee with a fresh perspective and new attitude to find a great solution.

There will always be times when a society, an economy, an industry, or a business changes radically and rapidly. The problems that emerge in such times may seem unsolvable. Yet despite the challenges they bring, these situations can hold enormous potential for individuals and companies alike. As I write this book, a serious recession is causing millions of people, and many businesses, to revise their goals and plans just to stay afloat. Yet even in the midst of this, new opportunities will arise. Some will miss those opportunities, focusing instead on the obstacles. But others—the wise—will focus on the *possibilities.* They will seize the opportunities, and in time, they will turn adversity into advantage and come out stronger than before.

An attitude that says, *I can achieve my objective despite the impediments in front of me* is absolutely the key. It provides the right frame of mind to spot opportunities during times of turmoil.

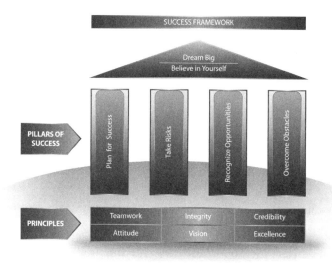

By approaching challenges with the right "principles," we create entirely new horizons that we otherwise might not explore. Focusing on the opportunities—places where you can not only solve the problem but also identify possibilities for growth in the process—is the key to making the impossible, possible. The graphic above shows you how I visualize the "pillars of success" and "principles" as a success framework for life.

Set Your Own Limits

Now, implicit in this discussion is the assumption that you have sufficient belief in your own abilities. This can be tough. Somewhere along the line you may have come to believe you weren't good at dealing with people or could never figure out marketing. Or you might be working for a boss who believes that you only have a certain set of skills.

Even in this case, the insight still holds true: never let others put limitations on what you can do. The moment you let them (or you do it yourself), you immediately close off a set of possibilities available to you.

Dream big and don't let anyone get in the way of that.

Is it all mind-set? No, you obviously need some skills. But assuming that you have them, attitude is the vital difference. In studying people who have faced tough situations, I have learned that when they fail, it is not because they lack the skills required to do the job successfully. They fail because they lack the insight to view the opportunities inside the problems that they are facing.

If you understand the opportunities, you can acquire the skills, or you can surround yourself with people who have the necessary skills. But there is no substitute for seeing the possibilities.

In the computer-capacity problem I described at the beginning of this chapter, skills were not an issue. We had some of our brightest people looking at the problem, yet they saw neither the solution nor the opportunity. It took someone with the right attitude—a positive one—to solve it. This kind of attitude is the number one determinant of success. When you have teams and team members who have positive attitudes and the necessary skills, then magic happens.

What I have learned in all these years of leading people is that if someone goes into a new project thinking he won't succeed, he usually doesn't. When I am thinking about assigning someone to a job, and he or she doubts that it can be done, I find someone else. Because if an individual goes into the project with a negative attitude, the odds of a positive result are very small.

If you watch basketball, you've seen players who go to the foul line not looking confident they can hit the shot. It's obvious in their body language. And sure enough, they miss. Expectations are a powerful predictor of outcomes. This is backed up by research that confirms the link between a positive mental attitude and surviving a difficult health diagnosis. Success is not assured, but the odds go way up when you believe you will win.

Looking for an Opening

Seeing the opportunity is not always easy. After all, when you are in a swamp, surrounded by alligators, your first thought is probably not, *You know, if we could just drain this thing and get rid of those gators, this would be a heck of a place to build a golf course.*

When you're faced with a very difficult situation, even surrounded with gators, you have to do two things. Obviously, first you must deal with the current reality. In our swamp example, you need to make sure you don't drown or get swallowed. But while you are dealing with the immediate crisis, you can do something else at the same time. Jim Collins talks about this in his book *Good to Great.* He advises focusing on the power of the *and*, not the limitations of the *or*.

In other words, at the same time you are dealing with the current reality, start developing a longer-term plan for how you're going to survive, succeed, and thrive by seizing the opportunities that are available to you within the situation you are facing.

The situation I inherited in Latin America is a textbook example. BellSouth Latin America had never turned a profit when I took over. My goal was to grow the business and make it profitable. But almost before I had time to introduce myself to all our employees, crisis was piling up on top of crisis. Just to recap: the Argentine economy collapsed, with a currency devaluation that took us from being a $1 billion company (in U.S. dollars) to a $250 million firm overnight.

In addition, due to disagreements, the partnership in Brazil did not make a payment on a billion-dollar loan. As a result, we had to negotiate with thirty-four banks simultaneously to try to work out a solution.

The Venezuelan economy went into turmoil when there was a coup attempt and Hugo Chavez was out of office for a couple of days. After he came back into power, businesses went on strike. There was no gasoline. There was no mail service. There were no bank services. Chaos reigned.

And in Colombia, rebels were blowing up our cell towers.

As we fought our way through those very immediate issues one by one, we never lost sight of the greater goal—growing the business and making it profitable. With that in mind, even though we were dealing with these terribly chaotic situations, I got the team together and told them that while we are trying to solve these individual problems, we still needed to look at the longer-term picture of what it was going to take for us to be successful in this region of the world.

By the time it was all done, we had turned the operation to profitability. And we did eventually accomplish our long-term goals. But it took both fighting the crises of the moment and also having a long-term plan and a long-term vision that would inspire people to work through those difficult challenges. Doing both was how we put lasting positive momentum behind the business.

Tough times of flux are all around us, in business and in every facet of life. Some call them "discontinuities"—times of change when things aren't going to be the way they were before. These times hold opportunities for those who see the possibilities and seize the day. These are situations to be embraced, not feared.

Most people run for safer ground, and as a result they miss out on what literally could be the opportunity of a lifetime. You should be running toward the chaos, looking for ways to make a difference. Plunge right in and take a risk, even though your instincts may tell you to do the opposite.

If I could give you a precise checklist of how to spot one of these times, I would do so. But that's not possible. Here are a few typical signs: rapid change from technological advancements (like broadband), new global marketplaces, new competitors, or new regulatory rules (the federal government eases restrictions on who can own what in communications). Opportunities abound in such developments.

But sometimes you're so close to the situation that you don't see the possibilities. Many of us remember when the Japanese first began exporting cars to the United States. Those cars were really inexpensive and not particularly known for their quality. So they were promptly dismissed by American car manufacturers. Over time those cars got better, and today Japanese cars are the ones to emulate. We may see history repeating itself with cars made in China. Initially, these cars are targeting the low-price segment, but does that mean they will focus there forever? Almost certainly not.

There are opportunities every day, especially with globalization. And the people who are really going to benefit are the ones who see them coming and get in early. Why don't others see the same thing? They don't take the broader view. They don't reflect on the meaning and implications of change. They don't stop to ask, "How big can this be?"

Searching for opportunities in every type of situation, and acting on those that you find, will accelerate your success. Expect some of them to appear in odd places and at inconvenient times—and be prepared to jump all over them.

Takeaway Messages

Inside every difficulty there is hidden opportunity.
The problems you encounter on your journey are
opportunities in disguise. You just have to dig
beneath the surface of the problem to find the
nugget (or nuggets) that can improve your life or
your organization's life.

Pivotal points represent great opportunities.
In turbulent times the decisions one makes can turn
adversity into advantage.

The "pillars of success" and the "principles"
that support them form a success framework
for life.

FOURTEEN

The Power of Sacrifice

Every great endeavor, whether personal or career, requires sacrifice. Perhaps it is easiest to understand this if you think about people who have turned a great vision into a reality. To me there is no better example of that than Dr. Martin Luther King Jr.

Dr. King had a bold vision: to eliminate racial injustice through nonviolent means. In order to achieve it, the people who accompanied him on his journey sacrificed and suffered a great deal. They were sprayed with fire hoses. They were beaten and incarcerated. Some were killed. But nothing could douse the desire for a better future that Dr. King instilled in his followers.

I see this as ultimate leadership: someone who inspires people to persevere even in the most extreme ordeals in order to fulfill a bold vision for a better future.

Think about it. Dr. King inspired people to march, sit in, and face the wrath of angry crowds, knowing they could be subjected to threats on their lives. Maybe you have to be a minority to understand how intimidating the situation was for his followers.

A small group being threatened by a larger group that has raw force on its side, plus the weight of authority. And yet this small group willingly took huge risks to change the future, not necessarily for themselves, but for their children and their children's children. To me, inspiring such behavior is leadership at its finest. The results show the power of sacrifice at work.

The fact that Dr. King was assassinated in the process of creating his vision underscores the degree of sacrifice he was willing to make. Major sacrifices, though usually not to the extent of giving up life itself, are always required to achieve something worthwhile.

Gears of Opportunity

We are an immigrant nation. Most of us are descended from people who gave up everything to come here. This country was born out of sacrifice, and it's maintained as a free country by the sacrifices that our military service personnel are making today. And obviously, I would not have had the chance to write this book without the sacrifices my parents made in deciding to come to this country.

Yet I don't remember ever reading a book on leadership where somebody said, to be successful you have to do a lot of sacrificing. It is not a popular subject. Many ears tend to close up when they hear the word. However, there is no denying the connection between sacrifice and success. The old adage "The harder I work, the luckier I get" comes to mind. This graphic shows what I mean.

In business, for example, when you are taking on a difficult task like a complicated merger, there's an incredible amount of work involved. The people trying to make it happen might spend months in hotel rooms. If you are involved in the project, you may have to sacrifice personal time and leisure time. In some cases you might not see your family for several weeks.

Why do it? Opportunity! In the case of the AT&T Wireless and Cingular merger, we knew we were involved in something special. We would be creating the nation's number one wireless company, capable of serving customers at a higher level and bringing new communications capabilities to the market. We knew we would be part of a landmark transaction, the largest all-cash corporate merger ever in the United States. We sacrificed to be a player in an historic moment. No one forced anyone to participate. Sacrifice is a personal choice.

We knew that when the merger happened, the people who

were going to comprise the AT&T Wireless–Cingular integration team would be working intensely for eight or nine months.
Before I had anyone sign on to the team, I asked a couple of
questions: "First, are you personally willing to take it on, with
the commitment it involves? Second, is your family in agreement? We don't know when this merger will be complete, but
whenever it happens, you will have to start work immediately.
You can't be vacationing in Europe when the FCC gives us the
approval. If you are, you need to take the very next plane back.
This takes priority. Can you and your loved ones deal with that?"
If a person had things going on in his or her personal life—like
a sick parent—that made it impossible to commit the necessary
time, we did not want that individual to be part of the team. We
did not want to place anyone in a position to have to choose
between the merger integration team and family.

Similar thought goes into choosing people to work for one of
our companies outside the States. They are going to pack up and
spend months out of the country. The ideal candidate is not a
parent with young kids in school. Better a single person or someone whose kids are in college or on their own. Someone free to
pick up and move. Someone eager for a new adventure and in a
good position in life to take it on.

As I think about it, I cannot come up with a single example
of a significant achievement that has occurred without sacrifice.
We live in a world that is truly flat. It's always 9 a.m. somewhere,
with a new workday getting started. In a globally interconnected
economy, the clock is always ticking. Competition is everywhere,
always on the move.

Are there some jobs that allow you to just work between 9 a.m. and 5 p.m.? Sure. But when you get to a certain level in business, you have to be willing to do what it takes to get the job done, and that means you will have to sacrifice upon occasion. We let our people know this is an expectation and requirement of aspiring leaders.

When I hired my chief of staff, we had an important conversation on this subject. I told her that there would be times when I would need her to work on Saturday to get something ready for Monday morning. I promised not to do this unless absolutely necessary, but it would sometimes happen, and I needed to know in advance that she would be okay with that. If some weekend work was unacceptable, she would not want the job.

The same can apply to others in the organization. If one of our cell sites goes down, customers don't want us to wait until next month, or even until 9 a.m. the next day, to fix it. They want service now. We must dispatch technicians to the cell site at midnight, if that's what it takes. (And we have to have the infrastructure to make that happen.)

People want to use their communications stuff at any time of the day, so a company like ours must respond. The peak time for our broadband usage is in the evening. Our stores are busiest on Saturday. So if you want your Saturdays and evenings off, don't apply to be a store manager.

None of this is about to slow down. If customers are more demanding—which they are, because they, too, are under time pressure—and they are more connected, then their reliance on those connections will increase. This means we must offer service calls on Sunday as well as Saturday, with extended hours during the week.

Entrepreneurs are the perfect example of sacrificing to create a better future. Many are willing to sacrifice everything they own, everything they have saved. I haven't found many entrepreneurs who only work from 9 a.m. to 5 p.m. on their venture. In fact, most work around the clock upon occasion, and in the case of a restaurant or small store, they might bring in the whole family to help.

A Generous Spirit

As you have seen from everything we have just talked about, sacrifice requires a generous spirit. You need to be unselfish, because the sacrifice you are making is usually for a greater cause. You are not the ultimate beneficiary. You may get great recognition or a raise if the sacrifice occurs in a workplace setting, but the benefits usually accrue to something far more important.

Let me use my own experience as an example. I have a very busy schedule at work. But I always try to take the time to go to a school and teach a Junior Achievement lesson or talk to students, because I believe I can inspire a student to achieve more than he or she might think possible otherwise. I may not ever see that child do it. But I truly believe it is worth the effort.

Clearly, I am not alone. There are a lot of people who donate their weekends or evenings—as well as their money—to a charitable or service organization. They do this because they think it will lead to positive change. A generous spirit allows you to give up time and resources to create value for others.

Generous spirits are everywhere, in every age group. My parents, like other immigrants, made a huge sacrifice, giving up everything they had—their possessions, their language, their culture, and their country, to go to a different place that they thought would be better for their children.

This is the real impetus for any sacrifice: the vision of a better future for yourself, your family, your friends, your community, and the world.

Inspiring Sacrifice at Work

It can be hard to motivate people to make this sort of sacrifice in business. For an executive, a big part of leadership is inspiring people to get involved in the mission of the company, encouraging them to do their best work. There is art in it. Quite frankly, I'm not aware of any business schools paying much attention to the subject. Maybe this will change in the future, because the topic is extremely important.

No one can force employees to sacrifice for the sake of a project, or a target, or even their team. They must feel that they are involved in a special cause so that when they look back in years to come, they will feel great pride in what they accomplished or helped to make happen. This goes back to the communication skills we have talked about that are so crucial to effective leadership of an organization.

Now, let me pause to make a point about long-term versus

short-term sacrifice in business. In business, sometimes you need to sacrifice to hit a long-term goal, but that does not mean you do it at the expense of the short-term goal. You have to do both. As we said earlier, it's about the *and*, not the *or*. Some people say it has to be one or the other. I've never accepted that. With a good plan and unrelenting effort, you can deliver both.

Sacrifice and Turnover

Whenever I talk about the importance of inspiring employee sacrifice, some people question if it is worth the effort. Most employees will have several jobs over the course of their lifetimes. Knowing this, executives often wonder, *Will my employees be here long enough and have enough vested in this company to be willing to sacrifice?*

I understand the point, but I think they are focusing on the wrong thing. The question is, why do people leave in the first place?

The reason most people have several employers over the course of a lifetime just might be that they never found the one job that inspired them to give their best. A leader's task is to show them a reason to stay by making the job more than a job.

Now, there are many, many people whose first passion is something outside of work. Maybe it's rescuing abused animals or teaching Sunday school or taking care of their family. We could not get along without these employees in our company. But wouldn't it be great to tap into some of that passion and help them be as excited about the impact they can make through their job as they are about life outside of work?

Personal Sacrifices

Perhaps the easiest place to understand the concept of sacrifice is in our personal lives. People intuitively sacrifice so their kids will have a better future. And many of us have sacrificed both money and time with our families in order to go back to school to further our careers.

Here's one of the most common examples of all. You have somebody who is doing well at work and is offered a huge promotion—and that prized assignment requires relocation. I've never seen a relocation that didn't involve sacrifice. You've got to give up your friends, and/or move away from your extended family. Your kids have to give up their friends. You pull up roots and start again. It can be traumatic.

That's a personal sacrifice. And it happens in the business world every day of the week. I think of it as a small version of the immigrant experience. You're leaving your community, your friends, your familiar scenes. Maybe you are going to a distant part of the country that has different slang, where you will feel like an outsider at first. So you are giving up everything that made you comfortable. Why? Because you believe there's a better future for you, and hopefully for your family, in doing so.

Every time I have moved, we've made it a family decision, and we've concluded that we are going to be better off as a family by moving than by staying behind. That's why, over time, we've moved from Miami to Chicago to Atlanta to San Antonio.

Whether personal or business, seeing the opportunity comes first, and then being willing to sacrifice to achieve it. As a manager of someone who is considering all of this, you want to make sure he or she sees all the positives. And that includes the whole family, since an unhappy spouse or children makes for a bad situation for the employee. Also, you want the individual to understand that future opportunities are not guaranteed if this one is turned down.

I don't judge a person who decides to stay put and hope for a future opportunity that works better for him or her. Transferring is a very personal thing. I respect the individual's decision. We'll just move on; it's not a problem.

It does get frustrating, however, when you know that making a sacrifice is the right career move for the person, and there is no reason not to do it. Young people with potential may not see the benefit of going back to college, when they are already getting a good paycheck. Why, they wonder, should they return to school full-time, or even part-time? It takes effort on your part to sell them on the need to do so.

Yet this is what leaders do. They reveal opportunity that others do not automatically see, and show them how it can change their future if they are willing.

Takeaway Points

To create anything of value, you must sacrifice.

Sacrifice must accompany a vision of a better future in order to be successful.

The more inspired you are about the brighter future, the more you are willing to sacrifice.

Sacrifice opens doors to opportunity, and hard work and discipline turn that opportunity into a reality.

FIFTEEN

Inclusion: It's About Making Heads Count

One of the best lessons I ever learned was in Ecuador while I was president of BellSouth Latin America. Alberto Sandoval, our general manager there, felt we could take our business to the next level by reorganizing the company along market segments: Cool (youth segment), Usted (professionals), and Alternativo/ Mi Gente (indigenous), instead of the one-size-fits-all approach we had been using.

The segmentation scheme was not controversial, but Alberto's plan to implement it raised a lot of eyebrows. He wanted to put people who represented the segments in charge of the segments. This meant we would have a very young person in charge of the youth segment. I was curious to see what would happen with a twenty-two-year-old running our marketing efforts to youth.

The young woman had plenty of ideas: brighter, hipper packaging; edgier advertising (more on this later in the chapter); and new distribution channels to reach the target consumer. These changes began to pay dividends right away. Our overall sales increased, and our short message service (SMS) text traffic began to soar. In fact, the results were so dramatic that we began to question the validity of the data. We rechecked it for accuracy. The numbers were right. Our youth business was going through the roof.

This experience confirmed that being willing to take an intelligent risk, in this case by elevating a talented young person into a decision-making role, can pay big dividends. Even more, it validated the wisdom of diversity and inclusion.

Looking and Thinking Like Customers

Successful companies connect with their customers. Think of the ones that do it best; people are proud to wear their logos like a badge of identity. One way to forge this kind of connection is to have a workforce that is representative of the customers you are trying to serve.

Who better than a young mother to sell to young mothers? If you are trying to reach eighteen- to thirty-five-year-old men, one of their peers will be more effective at selling to them than someone their grandfather's age. So, from a dealing-with-the-customer point of view, diversity makes sense. The people designing products, developing services, and dealing with your customers should be representative of the segments they serve.

Diversity makes a company (a) smarter, because you are getting different points of view; (b) more capable, because you are gaining additional skills; and (c) ultimately more profitable, because of (a) and (b) combined.

I believe that in today's marketplace, having a diverse workforce is a vital key to long-term success for any business. At Cingular, we saw an opportunity to capitalize on the fast growth of the Hispanic segment plus the fact that these consumers are heavy users of voice and data services. But when we looked at our internal capabilities, the truth was we didn't have sufficient bilingual staff. We had not developed bilingual advertising material, such as product brochures. And we didn't have a viable Spanish-language Web site.

To address these deficits, we hired a new executive director of Hispanic marketing, beefed up his staff, and increased his advertising budget so we could invest in sponsorships that are meaningful to Hispanic consumers. One of these was the Mexican National Soccer Team. Another was a group of TV shows including *Objetivo Fama*, the popular Spanish version of *American Idol*.

In markets with a large Hispanic population, we hired bilingual retail staff and other personnel. We made all of our marketing material available in Spanish as well as English. We got the Spanish Web site upgraded. These efforts were instrumental in making Cingular the top wireless carrier with Hispanic consumers.

The growth was so strong that we did some research to see which initiatives had the most impact. The results were interesting. If we added bilingual personnel and Spanish-language product information to a Cingular store in Hispanic markets, and made no other changes, sales would go up around 25 percent. These changes made people feel at home when they shopped at Cingular.

We had another breakthrough in a different area of diversity, with Cingular becoming the first wireless carrier to offer a phone with software for customers who are blind. One of our employees, Susan Palmer Mazrui, came up with this idea. Susan, who is legally blind, uses computer software that reads aloud information on her computer. She knew of similar software for wireless phones. It was a great idea, and we might have never thought of it except for having on our staff a representative of an underserved market segment. AT&T now offers a range of handsets with screen-reading and magnifying software plus specialized plans for people who are deaf. AT&T also worked with one of our vendors to develop a phone that addressed changes in vision, hearing, and cognition associated with aging as well as the preferences of an older market. It made Oprah Winfrey's 2008 list of top holiday gifts under one hundred dollars.

Diversity leads to an atmosphere of inclusion in which employees know that their ideas will be heard and respected. This is the key to encouraging fresh thinking and innovation. Diversity is not just about counting heads to make sure that certain numbers of certain groups are on the payroll. Diversity as a business strategy is about making heads count—giving a broad range of people the power to change how you do business.

Let's return to Cingular's intensification of Hispanic marketing. Some on our team pushed for increasing our Hispanic marketing talent at various rungs of the organization, but not necessarily at the top. Just increasing head count would not have accelerated our drive to leadership of this segment of the market. Instead, we went for an outstanding Hispanic marketing executive and invested him with real authority. That's how our business exploded with this market segment.

It's all about making heads count—leveraging the intelligence and ideas of a diversity of people whose backgrounds provide invaluable insight. The graphic below makes this clear.

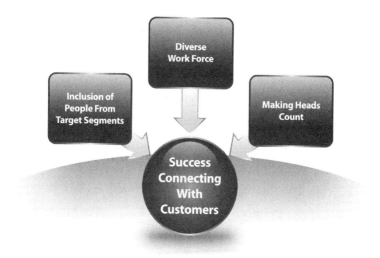

Connecting with Customers

Often, companies give lip service to diversity with the head-count approach, but they limit the real contributions because employee responsibility and accountability don't change. Not much changes with customers either. These companies forfeit the opportunity to develop new business with a particular segment of the market because they are not willing to make their diverse heads count.

Some people say we don't have to go the diversity route because smart marketers can sell to anyone. This was the thinking of some on my team about how to sell to Hispanics. They said it doesn't matter if they look the same as the market they are trying to serve.

After all, a man is running Mattel, a company that is best known for selling dolls. A woman is in charge of marketing at Harley-Davidson, a company known for selling to men.

There is no question that smart people can think outside the box of their own experience and background. But the odds are against you if you approach marketing without the insights of those who represent your target. It would be like a company making ski equipment with no employees who actually ski!

Sometimes the results of ignoring inclusion can be quite embarrassing. I remember an airline that did a Spanish-language ad heralding its new, more comfortable seats. The tagline in English was, "When you fly with us, you fly in leather." Worked just fine. But in Spanish, the literal translation was, "When you fly with us, you fly naked." Not the intended message. Not only was it an obvious mistake; it conveyed to Spanish-speaking consumers that the airline was putting on an act. It wanted their business but was not serious about taking steps to earn it. All it would have taken to avoid this mistake was a review of the ad by one Spanish-speaking individual.

Another unserious signal for Hispanic consumers is to take an ad created for English-speaking consumers and dub it into Spanish. These commercials never work as well as actually creating an ad for the intended audience. You will be much more successful if you rely on people who truly understand the segments you are trying to serve.

Now, I don't advocate rushing out tomorrow and adding inexperienced people just because they represent a particular customer segment. This is a long-term commitment to building a diverse workforce in which inclusion is prized.

I remember some years back reading about American car companies when they were starting to have problems. The article said their most senior executives couldn't believe all the complaints they were getting about their cars from their customers. But the executives were getting their own cars serviced by a professional staff. So the cars always were in top shape. The customer base wasn't getting the same treatment and had a very different perspective.

Without a workforce that is representative of your customers, you can be equally out of touch. The ideal environment is one in which a twenty-five-year-old can talk about how to sell to other twenty-five-year-olds and is given serious consideration. It needs to be inclusive of ideas as well as different types of people.

This really hit home with me when Cingular was considering developing a phone specifically for the youth market. We had a big, deep discussion because the concept was controversial. The people who convinced me we needed to develop this phone were the team members who were mothers of teens and pre-teens. They emphasized that from a mother's point of view, one of the most difficult things is not being able to communicate with her kids. They kept asking me, "Ralph, do you know how hard that is?" And I had to say no. I'm not a mother, and my two sons are grown. But I heard the emotion in the room, and it convinced me.

The phone sold very well—much better than I had expected.

That's the payback you get for listening to a diverse group in which people feel free to contribute their ideas and opinions.

Heads Count When Individuals Matter

Inclusion also means giving team members the leeway to be their best, on their own terms. In Latin America, I was at a meeting listening to proposals for projects that needed funding. An engineer representing our Ecuador business got up to make his presentation. He started in English because some of our staff were based in the States and didn't speak Spanish. For this guy, English was very difficult. He was having an awful time, and it was painful listening to him. So in the middle of his presentation, I asked him if he would prefer to do it in Spanish. Which he did.

In his own language, he was super-eloquent—just brilliant. We approved funding for the project, which never would have happened if he had continued in English. We would have judged him based on his faulty performance in a language he rarely used. The problem wasn't him so much as our biases about what constituted a proper presentation.

Ever since, I try to be on guard against similar situations that are really nothing more than prejudice about how a person looks or sounds.

Remember the episode in Ecuador that I mentioned earlier, when we installed a twenty-two-year-old as marketing director for our youth segment? I didn't like the look of her ads. I didn't like the music she wanted to use. I didn't like the graphics.

But I approved it anyway. I wasn't the target, and I was smart enough to say, "All I'm going to judge is the results." On that basis, I liked all of it very, very much!

Inclusion as a Personal Commitment

An African-American friend of mine told me a great story that brings home how blind spots can pervade (and pervert) our thinking. He was one of our top executives, and he had just moved to a new house in a very nice neighborhood. On a Saturday he was washing his car in the driveway. His new next-door neighbor came over and asked him how much he charged. The neighbor assumed that a black man washing a car in front of a nice house had been hired for the job. How awkward is that?

In our personal life, and in business, everything goes better with an open attitude, avoiding judgment based on how people look or talk. In my own case, I am not a tall guy. Since I'm not a basketball player, what does it matter? I tell people you shouldn't measure people by their stature; you should measure them on the power of their ideas.

Takeaway Messages

If your workforce looks like your customer base, your organization will be more successful.

Creating an inclusive environment is not about counting heads, it's about making heads count.

So **create an environment that makes contributing easy.** This means discarding prejudices about the way people look, talk, or dress.

SIXTEEN

Make the Journey About More than You

One international effort I was proud to sponsor was the BellSouth Proniño (Pro-Child) Initiative. I championed this effort while president of BellSouth's wireless operations in eleven countries in Latin America in coordination with the BellSouth Foundation.

In Latin America, it is estimated that as many as twenty-one million children in the region are working instead of attending school. You see these children selling flowers in the streets, shining shoes, or taking care of their brothers and sisters so their parents can work. Since they do not get a proper education, their future is limited.

Proniño was a six-million-dollar, five-year program we funded to address the problem. It provided scholarships that covered tuition, books and supplies, uniforms, transportation, meals, tutoring, and family counseling. In some cases a small stipend was provided to families to help offset the economic loss of having the child attend school rather than working. This approach broke the vicious cycle of poverty and provided these children with the opportunity to reach their full potential. The program was successfully launched in Guatemala, Panama, Nicaragua, Venezuela, Colombia, Peru, Ecuador, Chile, Argentina, and Uruguay. As a result of BellSouth Proniño, more than seven thousand children returned to the classroom.

Once you get to a certain level, no matter what profession you're in, you have a responsibility to help others. Perhaps because of my background, I have always felt a great sense of obligation to give back. But no matter where you come from, or how you grew up, helping others is the right thing to do.

One of many reasons to give back is that others will notice and want to do the same. Eventually all of these efforts could change our communities and the lives of people who live there for the better.

If somebody had not helped me as a ten-year-old immigrant alone in the United States, I would not be where I am today. I was caught by a really strong safety net, a safety net of people who helped me enormously in those rough early days. There was the Baez family that took me in. Classmates who helped me learn the English language. The Cuban community in Miami. That strong support system made the difference for countless Cuban immigrants like my family and me. Often, all people need is just a little help to get going so they can succeed on their own.

Sometimes when I say this, people respond, "But charity begins at home. You have to make sure that you and your loved ones are taken care of." And I agree. Charity should begin at home, but from there it can spread to many other places. Once you reach a certain point in your journey, you realize that life is about more than personal gain. You get to a place where you understand how rewarding it is to help others on their journey.

People who have made it should feel this obligation. That's something I believe strongly. As the saying goes, in the end you can't take it with you. There is a reason hearses don't come with luggage racks. It's a shame when a person doesn't realize this until it's too late to make a difference for someone else.

Many people wait until they are older to start giving their wealth away. That is the path Warren Buffet is taking. He is now giving back in an incredible way to charity. But why wait? Give a little back as early as you can. Donate money as you are able. Donate time, which can be even more impactful. Do it at a point when you will have many years left to see the effects of your giving. Build into your life the practice of helping others.

All of us belong to communities. When we build them up, we benefit ourselves, our families, our neighbors, and the future. And in the process, we make interesting contacts. We get into networks and learn about different perspectives that broaden our horizons. So in helping others, we enrich ourselves. It's not a one-way street.

This work can teach us a lot. People can't be ordered to give of themselves on behalf of helping others. But we can coach and inspire them in this direction. It requires a unique set of skills to motivate people to do a thing for the sheer goodness of doing it. Developing this ability will make you more successful at work at the same time it leaves you more fulfilled in daily life.

Giving Back

Notice the elements in the graphic below. Giving back is at the center, complemented by having a passion to help, volunteering, and mentoring.

Passion is a good starting point. Pick something you believe in deeply. The environment. Education. Fighting hunger. Finding a cure for a disease. There is no lack of important causes. Choose one that's important to you, get involved, and make a difference. Why not leave a legacy? When you look back on your life, one of the things you may be proudest of is what you did to help others.

I'm a great believer in leaving a legacy by mentoring people who will follow in your path. In our company we hold mentoring sessions, and I try to pass on the lessons I have learned on my journey and have shared in this book. Mentoring can be highly effective in helping others navigate the pathway to success.

I do mentoring in many different ways. If someone asks me, I will work one-on-one with him or her. I have also mentored groups like our women's employee network over lunch. I've used a similar approach with Hispanics and other groups. I have even done "e-mentoring" over the Internet. All of these methods can be effective. The key is to commit to do them.

You don't need to be a CEO to be an effective mentor. Many people bring experiences and knowledge that others can learn from. We encourage our managers to mentor, although we don't force it since not everyone is good at it. It's a personal decision.

Typically the attendees at these mentoring sessions are a mix of employees of various levels from numerous business units. The leaders are volunteers. Some people like an open discussion, some have specific agendas, and some mentors give their mentees homework to do.

My typical approach to mentoring is to take recent events and discuss their implications for our company and/or community. I always ask the mentee group what issues or topics they would like to include in the discussion. The resulting interaction is dynamic, real-time, and personal. I draw from experiences from my life and career to help employees think about how to deal with the event or situation. This isn't the only way to mentor; it's just one of many approaches that can work well.

Mentoring is different from developing people, which is more formal. Development has a curriculum, assessments, and a defined path of training, education, and experience. Mentoring is more ad hoc, sharing what you have learned in your career so others can do better in theirs. It's informal, less structured. Mentoring is a nice complement to development, but it doesn't supplant that process.

Leaders Touch the Community

The concepts of developing people and helping your community tie together. Leaders help others reach their full potential, and they also help the community improve as a volunteer engaged in socially responsible practices and actions.

A socially responsible action could be helping the local United Way or some other group raise funds for what your community needs. You do this because you believe the result will help create a better place for you and your family to live.

Many people become passionate about a cause because it represents something that has touched them. Perhaps someone in their family has been impacted by a disease. So whether it's breast cancer or diabetes or autism, they work incredibly hard to help find a cure.

The disease you fight might be an infection in the community, such as gangs or crime. There are any number of things that make people want to sacrifice and do something socially responsible. They run marathons to raise money. Or they walk or bike or paint houses. Why? Because they want to help make their community better and believe their contribution will make this happen.

All of this ties to our earlier discussion about the importance of sacrifice. Often, people are willing to sacrifice for the sake of giving back because they think there's something valuable in it down the road.

Of course, some say, "Not me" or, "No time." Then they find themselves living in South Florida when Hurricane Andrew hits and destroys everything, and suddenly people who could never imagine being homeless are living in a shelter for a while because their home was destroyed. It happens. And when it does, you are really glad that someone sacrificed so you could benefit.

Where and how you choose to get involved is up to you. What do you feel strongly about? Put your money, time, and energy there.

I believe giving back doesn't have to be as prescriptive as tithing or following a certain rule. But in some form, it needs to happen. Everyone owes somebody who helped them out. Companies owe the community that supports their business. We all owe each other.

My Passions

Two causes that I am passionate about are Junior Achievement, which I discussed earlier, and the Boy Scouts. What they have in common is a commitment to helping kids have a better life and reach their full potential.

The Boy Scouts do this by inspiring youth with the right values. They teach boys how to win the right way. The principles the Boy Scouts teach are captured in the Scout Oath, which is also known as the Scout Promise:

On my honor. I will do my best
to do my duty to God and my country
and to help obey the Scout Law:
To help other people at all times;
to keep myself physically strong,
mentally awake, and morally straight.

This oath, when combined with the Scout Motto of "Be prepared" and the Scout Slogan of "Do a good turn daily," provides a moral compass to guide over 4.6 million young people worldwide.

JA helps kids have a better life through financial education and job shadowing. Around the world, JA teaches over eight million students financial literacy and entrepreneurship, preparing them to enter the workforce and succeed.

Why these two organizations? Education is a big part of what made me the person I am. If I had not listened to my grandmother when she said, "Ralph, save your money and go to school," my life would have been far different. I would have been a good airplane mechanic, but I don't think I'd be in a position to write a book.

The message my grandmother gave me is the same message I give kids through JA: stay in school, get a good education, and the sky is the limit in terms of what you'll be able to accomplish. It was grandmother's comments that really got me started going to schools and talking to kids, especially Hispanic kids, because they have such a high dropout rate. According to the EPE Research Center, in a study released in June 2008, only 58 percent of Hispanic students entering the ninth grade made it to graduation four years later (according to data on the 2005 graduating class, the latest available). In other words, 42 percent dropped out of high school.

I don't see how anyone cannot be moved by this situation, especially if you have a minority background. I could have been one of those kids. I could have dropped out.

But it takes more than school to succeed. Without the right values, bad things happen. So in addition to the educational emphasis of JA, I admire how the Boy Scouts give young people the right foundation for developing character. I've never seen a better organization for teaching values to kids than the Scouts.

I first got involved with JA and the Boy Scouts in South Florida. Junior Achievement recruited me to be on their board in Miami. I didn't know much about them at the time. But once I got a taste of what they did, I said, "This makes all the sense in the world."

JA teaches kids by engaging them in experiences that make the learning process fun and engaging. In one exercise, the students run a mythical company. They have to make payroll, sell products, and make a profit—all the things that make the business world go round.

Another activity is called JA Finance Park. Here you play the role of an individual in the local business community. You are assigned a source of employment. It is interesting to listen to some of the kids when given a role with a low-paying job. Some complain, "I can't live on what you're paying me." Well, guess what? That's the real world. And when you only have so much money in the checkbook, you need to make difficult choices. You need to find a way to make ends meet.

Observing this exercise, I can see lightbulbs start to turn on. Some well-off kids who never considered balancing a checkbook or earning extra money start to think about such things. Other kids from homes where there are not a lot of extras begin to see the value of staying in school and preparing for the life they dream of. The most striking thing about watching kids go through JA or the Boy Scouts is the change in perspective. They start to see the world in a different way. They are on a path to becoming better members of society.

Of course, a few are harder to reach. One day I was teaching a JA class to help students see themselves as entrepreneurs, building their own business. The assignment was for each kid to create a business card that reflected the work that he or she wanted to do. All types were represented—construction, catering, fashion design, and so on. But there was one student who refused to be engaged. He sat in the back and didn't participate. I tried to involve him, but he insisted he wasn't interested in any type of work or business.

"What do you like to do?" I asked him. "Nothing," was his reply. We went back and forth like this for several minutes. I kept pressing him until he finally thought of one thing he liked doing—sleep. So we determined that his vocation could be "mattress tester." He created a business card for an imaginary company named sleep.com and gave himself the title of Chief Mattress Tester!

The great majority of students have real enthusiasm for the idea of becoming a self-made success. It is fun to watch this. You see a kid who didn't grow up with much suddenly understand that he might be able to start his own company. And when kids leave a JA session, they're jazzed. Why? Because they're not in the classroom, getting a lecture from the teacher; they are learning about business for themselves. It is real.

I had the same reaction when I got involved with Boy Scouts. When they were recruiting me to serve on their board, I got to meet a few of the kids they helped, boys who had gone from being a gang member to achieving the highest rank of Eagle Scout. If you're an Eagle Scout, you've shown you are a pretty special and rare person. When I saw the changes Boy Scouts made in these kids, I wanted to get involved.

Getting our young people interested in learning and inspired to work hard is critical to their future success and to society as a whole. *The Silent Epidemic: Perspectives of High School Dropouts* is an alarming report released in 2006 by Civic Enterprises, a public policy firm that helps corporations, nonprofits, foundations, universities, and governments develop innovative ideas to strengthen communities and the country. It says that nearly half (47 percent) of the dropouts surveyed said a major reason they left school was that classes were not interesting. And nearly seven out of ten (69 percent) said they were not motivated or inspired to work hard.[1]

Several years earlier, a report on the 2003–2004 class in Atlanta showed that less than 60 percent graduated from high school. For Hispanic students in Georgia, the numbers are even lower. I was a resident of Georgia at the time. This alarming news was a call to action that resulted in the formation of the Junior Achievement (JA) of Georgia Hispanic Outreach Initiative.

The JA of Georgia Hispanic Outreach Initiative

The JA of Georgia Hispanic Outreach Initiative addresses the challenges facing young Hispanics that keep them from reaching their full potential: language barriers, economic barriers, acculturation barriers, and lack of role models.

The program provides experiential, activity-based programs taught by Hispanic businessmen and -women (non-Hispanics also teach these classes with special job aids) who act as role models for students, imparting their knowledge and encouraging them to complete their education.

I am proud to have served as chairman of the JA of Georgia Hispanic Outreach Initiative from its inception in 2002 until 2006. Together with Donna Buchanan, the energetic former president of JA of Georgia, and Kat Delgado, the talented director of the Hispanic Outreach Initiative, we recruited other Hispanic leaders in the community and major corporations such as GE, UPS, and Home Depot, who joined the ranks of Cingular Wireless and BellSouth (now part of AT&T) to expand the initiative.

The results have been amazing. In 2003 we began the program with 50 volunteers and reached 547 students. In 2007, the program included more than 700 volunteers who touched the lives of more than 10,000 students.

The JA of Georgia Hispanic Initiative was recently evaluated by a third party, and the findings confirmed excellent results. Here are just two highlights:

- 95 percent of participants said they were inspired to be successful in the future.

- 98 percent said they would recommend the program to a friend.

The JA of Georgia Hispanic Outreach Initiative has been so successful that JA Worldwide has agreed to launch the program nationwide with the support of the Goizueta Foundation. I am now chairman of the Hispanic Outreach Initiative for JA Worldwide, and we have expanded the initiative to New York, Denver, Los Angeles, Chicago, San Francisco, and New Mexico.

This is an example of what can be accomplished when business leaders partner with the local community to improve the lives of its citizens. And the efforts to improve our communities don't need to stop at our borders. They can be successfully implemented anywhere in the world.

The more successful you are in business, the more you should feel an obligation to give back. That's why I get involved with JA and the Boy Scouts and have championed efforts like the BellSouth Proniño initiative. I feel a greater urgency to give something back now than when I was a young engineer. In part it is because I have been successful, and in part it is because I know there are many young people who need a helping hand to get started on the right path to fulfill their potential.

Find the cause that sparks real passion in your soul, and make it part of who you are.

Takeaway Messages

Leaders help people reach their full potential.
That is one of a leader's most important jobs.

Leaders also help communities reach their full potential. No one—neither an individual nor a business—exists in a vacuum. We have an obligation to give back. I have seen the power that just a small amount of help or encouragement can have on a young person's life. Mine.

Great leaders make a great impact in their communities.

SEVENTEEN

Become the Leader You Want to Be

At a time when operations managers in telecommunications were nearly all male, I assigned a very capable female manager to run our operations in a district in Alabama. I made a point of checking back frequently to see how she was doing, including asking the technicians she supervised. One by one, they gave glowing reports. When I asked why they thought she was so good, I kept getting the same answer: "She fixed the gate."

This particular operation had a work center that was located in a desolate area, and for quite a while before she took over, the automatic gate to the property had been broken. This left the property vulnerable to break-ins and thefts. Previous managers had not attended to the problem. She dealt with it immediately and earned instant respect and appreciation.

Nothing communicates leadership like decisions and actions that show what you believe is important. Knowing where to focus is paramount.

Assessing Where You Are

We have talked throughout the book about setting goals and establishing ways to assess your progress toward reaching them. The logical question to ask from time to time is, Where am I on the journey toward my goals?

Clearly, when it comes to your personal goals, it is fairly easy to find out. If your goal is to save $250,000 and you have $175,000 put away, you are 70 percent there. If you want to earn a high school diploma and you've completed your junior year, you're three-fourths of the way to graduation. If you want to be an executive vice president of your organization and you are an assistant vice president today, then you know there are steps left to take before you can reach your goal.

But when it comes to determining the skills you have acquired on your journey, measurement is more amorphous. How do you know you've arrived at your goal when it's not immediately apparent? That is why I created the Leadership Capability Model, which is based on more than thirty years of management experience.

The Leadership Capability Model

The Leadership Capability Model defines five increasingly sophisticated levels of leadership ability. Before we look at these levels individually, there are a couple of things to note about the model in general.

First, the levels build upon each other. For example, the

Experiential Level (Level 1) describes the initial learnings that are the foundation of a leader's set of beliefs and values.*

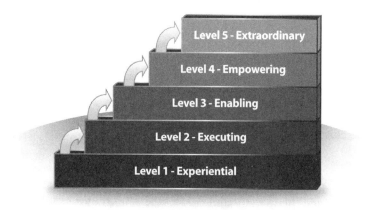

Second, it is clear that all five steps build off the concepts we have mentioned previously in the book.

Let's look at each level more closely.

Level 1: Experiential. This is the beginning of your leadership journey. You learn from every experience and begin to form the beliefs and values that you will carry with you throughout your career. The focus at this level is on self-development and individual accomplishment in the context of what the organization is trying to accomplish.

---

* These core beliefs and values don't change; they guide your day-to-day actions. But in advanced levels, you learn that sometimes you need to adapt to world changes by finding new ways to move toward your goal. While remaining true to your principles, you may have to unlearn old ways of doing things and find new ways to respond more effectively to a changing world.

You will recall my experience at Bellcore TEC in Illinois (Pivotal Point 2). My essential learning there was the importance of creating a powerful vision that energizes and motivates people to achieve extraordinary results. Ever since this key experience in my career, I have focused on making sure any organization I was a part of had a clear and inspiring vision.

Key characteristics: experiencing new things, reflecting and learning from those experiences, and then applying those learnings.

Level 2: Executing.

The second level of the model is characterized by focus on execution, always grounded in values and morals. In this stage the leader demonstrates the importance of integrity and credibility. These two building blocks are essential to the development of future leadership skills and capabilities and also to earn the respect of both peers and superiors.

A key Level 2 learning for me came during my assignment as president of BellSouth Internet and Broadband Services, which confirmed that you can have both great integrity and great results when you do the right things in the right way.

Key characteristic: consistently doing the right thing and delivering results.

Level 3: Enabling.

In the first two levels, the focus is on individual contribution and doing the right things. The third level is defined by enabling the people who work for you to execute the organization's strategies and initiatives. The big idea here is to help others reach their full potential while still delivering the results you are responsible for. In the aftermath of Hurricane Andrew, chaos characterized the operating environment my team was facing. Establishing small teams and giving them unusual latitude within a strategic framework was how we restored the network.

Key characteristics: encouraging others and creating winning teams.

Level 4: Empowering. One of a leader's most important jobs is to grow other leaders. In Level 4 the leader empowers others to execute the organization's strategies and initiatives, always understanding that the leader himself or herself retains ultimate responsibility. My experience with BellSouth Latin America (my Pivotal Point 5) was a case of establishing a shared vision while empowering country managers to execute effectively in their own markets. We turned our business around in spite of all the unusual external obstacles.

Key characteristics: setting clear direction and expectations for the people who work for you.

Level 5: Extraordinary. This is the ultimate leadership level. Few leaders reach this level where stellar results are consistently achieved. Level 5 leaders create compelling visions that are shared by the organization, while growing personally through the beliefs and values that they acquired through their leadership journey.

In my own career, the best example of achieving extraordinary results came during my tenure at Cingular Wireless (now AT&T Mobility). I was fortunate to work with Stan Sigman, whom I mentioned earlier, and an incredible team of leaders who defied the odds to execute one of the most successful large-scale business merger integrations ever in any industry (my Pivotal Point 6). We delivered extraordinary results in customer growth, revenue growth, and margin growth when industry analysts had predicted we would lose customers following the merger. This is a clear case in which an inspiring vision, a sound plan, and a strong focus on execution led to extraordinary results.

Key characteristics: inspiring others to achieve more than they thought possible.

Let's summarize all five levels in a table that you can use to chart your progress toward your own leadership goals.

Level	Stage	Leadership Capabilities
1	Experiential	Understands the organization's vision Learns from leadership experiences and adapts to new situations Develops beliefs set and principles Executes the organization's strategies, initiatives, and overall plan Works with teams to deliver results Develops self and provides coaching and feedback to others
2	Executing	Develops plan to achieve vision Delegates responsibility to execute strategies, initiatives, and the overall plan Selects the right people and assigns accountability Monitors implementation of plans and removes roadblocks Creates a winning environment and relationships

3	Enabling	Communicates vision and helps others understand it Enables others to execute strategies, initiatives, and the overall plan Overcomes resistance to change Develops people and creates development opportunities Delivers results and internalizes key measures Recognizes and rewards high performance
4	Empowering	Owns vision and helps others to own it Internalizes values and lives by them Empowers others to execute strategies, initiatives, and the overall plan Motivates people to achieve results Exceeds expectations defined by key measures and timetables Recognizes and rewards high performance
5	Extraordinary	Creates a compelling vision of the future Establishes values and lives by them Selects strategies and key initiatives and oversees the overall plan to achieve vision Establishes goals and priorities and focuses the organization Aligns and inspires people to achieve bold goals Establishes key measures and timetables and monitors results Creates a winning culture and then selects and develops leaders to sustain it

The Leadership Capability Model in Action

In my career I have observed and worked with many great leaders, and I've also studied the leadership practices of some of the great figures of history. My conclusion is that the very best of them concentrate in ten areas. This is how they make a difference.

To bring the fifth and ultimate level of the Leadership Capability Model to life, let's take a look at someone who was, indeed, an extraordinary leader in all ten of these areas. As I mentioned earlier, I regard Dr. Martin Luther King Jr. as an exceptional example of leadership. Following is a list of the ten most important, high-impact behaviors of leadership, and an illustration of their use by Dr. King, one of the most compelling leaders of recent history.

Leaders

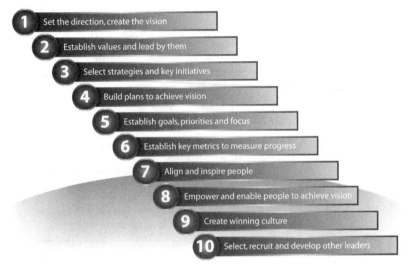

1 Set the direction, create the vision

2 Establish values and lead by them

3 Select strategies and key initiatives

4 Build plans to achieve vision

5 Establish goals, priorities and focus

6 Establish key metrics to measure progress

7 Align and inspire people

8 Empower and enable people to achieve vision

9 Create winning culture

10 Select, recruit and develop other leaders

First—*Set the Direction, Create the Vision*

People look to the leader of an organization—a business, church, or nonprofit organization—to provide vision from which actions will emerge. Some people don't like the word *vision* because it sounds abstract. Fine. Call it establishing an agenda or the ultimate goal. But no matter what you call it, you need to do it.

Really good leaders create a shared vision, one that inspires others in the organization to believe and makes them willing to sacrifice to make it a reality. And note that it is usually the work of one leader. I have yet to see a leadership committee work effectively.

While Dr. King relied on a circle of trusted advisers to fulfill many key responsibilities, no one doubted that he was the source of the inspirational vision for the civil rights movement. His "I Have a Dream Speech," delivered in Washington, D.C., on August 28, 1963, in front of 250,000 people, articulated his vision for America.

Dr. King clearly communicated his vision (his dream) by tying it to the American dream articulated in the Declaration of Independence. In doing so he spoke to the aspirations of the people he represented in a clear and inspiring way. That inspiration was necessary because he knew they would have to sacrifice to have a better future. He said, "We must face the difficulties of today and tomorrow." Dr. King internalized and personalized his vision by including how one day his children would live the dream.

Leaders who can persuade others to act on a shared vision of the future create a powerful force and a unifying bond—two key ingredients to overcoming obstacles and achieving difficult goals.

Second—*Establish Values and Lead by Them*

Almost as important as setting the agenda is establishing the values and beliefs the organization is going to follow. Leaders must model the behavior they want their organization to exhibit. If your goal is to have an organization of the highest integrity, you need to hire people who embody it and create a culture (see point 9 below) to sustain those values.

Dr. King developed his nonviolence philosophy and values as an integral part of his leadership journey. After the historic Montgomery bus boycott—when blacks in Alabama stopped riding the city's buses after Rosa Parks, a black woman, was arrested for refusing to give up her seat to a white male passenger—Dr. King was asked to chronicle the movement so that others could use it as blueprint for their future efforts.[1] The result was the book *Stride Toward Freedom: The Montgomery Story*. In it, he refined his leadership values.

> When I went to Montgomery as a pastor, I had not the slightest idea that I would later become involved in a crisis in which non-violent resistance would be applicable. . . . Living through the actual experience of the protest, non-violence became more than a method to which I gave intellectual assent; it became a commitment to a way of life.[2]

The civil rights movement in general, and the Montgomery incident specifically, were clearly pivotal points for Dr. King. As a result, he not only further developed his philosophy and values, but he also learned how to internalize them and live by them—something that all extraordinary leaders have in common.

Third—*Set Strategies and Key Initiatives*

It's impossible to do everything. Leaders choose a fixed (and relatively small) number of strategies to follow and tell people in a clear, concise, and consistent fashion how to accomplish them. If you constantly change either the strategies or the key initiatives, people are going to get confused, and nothing will get done.

In pursuit of the civil rights movement's clear and well-defined mission, Dr. King understood the need for organization, planning, and goal setting. He held frequent meetings before, during, and after each mobilization event. After the first successful day of the Montgomery bus boycott, which he called the Day of Days (December 5, 1955), Dr. King realized that the movement could not continue without more careful planning. So he established a finance committee to raise money in order to fund the movement. He also established a program committee to plan regular mass meetings and a strategic committee to get the best minds to think through the issues and make recommendations to the executive board of the Montgomery Improvement Alliance.[3]

Under his leadership, the movement skillfully refined strategies and tactics as necessary in order to sustain the boycott in Montgomery. Their swift yet organized actions successfully maintained the boycott for 381 days until the U.S. Supreme Court declared that Alabama's state and local laws requiring segregation in buses was unconstitutional.

The Montgomery boycott changed the history of the civil rights movement and launched Dr. King in the national spotlight.

Fourth—*Build Plans to Achieve the Vision*
Planning logically follows from setting strategies, but you would be amazed at how many people forget to create a plan in their

haste to get underway. The plan needs to be written down and constantly referred to. It should serve as a compass, a beacon, that helps people stay on track. (And if you can create and execute a multiyear plan, you have made it to the big leagues. You don't get anywhere overnight.)

The leaders of the Southern Christian Leadership Conference, with Dr. King at the head, planned with a long-term and large-scale view. The Birmingham campaign is a good example of the strategic nature of their efforts. In 1963 the SCLC responded to Rev. Fred Shuttlesworth's request for assistance in Birmingham by devising a plan—but not just for the moment and not just for one city. They thought in terms of the nation.[4] The Albany Movement in Georgia during the summer of 1962 had provided Dr. King with important lessons that were used in Birmingham the following year.

The plan for the Birmingham campaign called for the desegregation of lunch counters, restrooms, and water fountains. It also called for the hiring of blacks in local businesses and industry and the formation of a biracial committee to work out a timetable for desegregation of other areas of the city.[5] The reason for the timeline was to give the other side a face-saving way to back down. A key aspect of the plan was to go to Birmingham with trained leaders to maintain discipline despite the violence they would encounter. The demonstrators would also be prepared for the harsh conditions in jail. They would pack toothbrushes, layered clothing, and other necessary items.[6]

Devising plans and actions to overcome incredible odds was a hallmark of Dr. King's leadership style. He had the ability to adapt to the constantly changing situations and obstacles he and his movement faced. Learning how to overcome obstacles is an essential quality of extraordinary leadership, and Dr. King excelled at it.

Fifth—*Establish Goals, Priorities, and Focus*

These should be stretch goals—requiring some effort to achieve. Of course they will mesh with what the organization is trying to accomplish.

Dr. King believed: (a) goals must be clearly stated, (b) the simplest approach will prove to be the most effective, and (c) one should never aim too low.[7]

He set goals around which people could unite. During the early years of the struggle (1955–1957), his main objectives included securing basic human dignity—the ability to drink from any public water fountain—and the right to vote. In 1960 the goal was to desegregate all public eating facilities. In 1965 it was to abolish voting restrictions, poll taxes, and police brutality.[8]

This attention to establishing goals, setting priorities, and focusing the organization is the hallmark of great leadership.

Sixth—*Establish Key Metrics to Measure Progress*

You need to know if your organization is staying on track with respect to your goals. Simple, visible metrics help people stay on course.

Again, the Birmingham campaign provides a good illustration from Dr. King's leadership career. He and his staff set specific goals and deadlines. They wanted stores desegregated by a certain date;

fair hiring practices established by a fixed deadline following that; and the establishment of a biracial committee to monitor and enforce the implementation of city desegregation after the first two goals were accomplished.[9]

Great leaders not only define the goals and objectives for their organizations, but they also provide a clear way to measure results and track progress, knowing that even the best plans will need to change as circumstances change.

Seventh—*Align and Inspire People*

This piece often gets missed by people who are concentrating on execution and metrics. That's a mistake. You need to make sure your people are aligned with the goals you have established in order to make sure they are going to achieve the right things. If the play is to run the ball to the right, your people need to know they need to block to the right.

Changing the metaphor a bit, the role of the leader is like an orchestra conductor. Getting individual employees to work in concert doesn't just happen. Alignment leads to beautiful harmony and synchrony.

Few orators could match Dr. King's ability to inspire people to rally around a shared vision. His best-known speeches, "I Have a Dream" and "I See the Promised Land," were full of metaphors and imagery that not only expressed hope but helped people to focus on the task at hand. Great leaders persuade and inspire people to fulfill the shared vision. They do not coerce or force their mission on people. That never works in the long term.

The Birmingham campaign became a pivotal point in Dr. King's leadership journey by showing his ability to influence and inspire, not only his followers, but the rest of the world. Soon after the campaign began, the city of Birmingham obtained an injunction against his demonstrations. Leveraging the lessons of Albany, Dr. King was determined to not let an injunction deter him. He decided to go to jail and join demonstrators who were already there for violating the injunction. This decision and his famous letter from the Birmingham jail rallied people throughout the world to his cause. In the letter he addressed the court injunction by writing, "There are two types of laws, just and unjust. One has a moral responsibility to disobey unjust laws." He then went on to define an unjust law as "a human law that is not rooted in eternal law and natural law. All segregation statues are unjust because segregation distorts the soul and damages the personality."[10]

Dr. King persuaded people by deed and word. He got them to see that a nonviolent path was the right course to take, both morally and ethically. Convinced and inspired, people embraced his ideas with commitment and conviction. There can be no greater testament to a leader.

Eighth—*Empower and Enable People to Achieve the Vision*

Once people are aligned, then you want to empower and enable them within the framework you set so they become instrumental in achieving the organization's goals.

Dr. King believed in developing leaders through training

and sharing responsibility. To enable and empower others, he established a Leadership Training Committee that provided intensive training for participants in the nonviolence movement. Workshops on nonviolence taught people to tolerate harsh language and the physical abuse they might face if they took part in the demonstrations.[11] Eventually a facility was established to create "non-commissioned officers of the civil rights movement." Volunteers from across the country came to learn nonviolent techniques as well as specific areas of expertise, like conducting voter-registration drives.[12] Dr. King's plan deliberately included the cultivation of dedicated people who would propel the movement over the long term, and this was one of his great successes.

Ninth—*Create a Winning Culture*

The first eight points allow an organization to succeed. The last two on the list address the need to sustain success. A winning culture communicates what the organization values. People don't get it from reading the personnel manual. They get it from each other, from observing the kind of behavior that is encouraged and rewarded, showing what the organization truly believes.

Through Dr. King's leadership, the civil rights movement became a culture in and of itself—a magnetic force drawing people of talent and energy. Dr. King was skilled at choosing the right people to build a winning culture—leaders like Andrew Young and Ralph D. Abernathy, who helped shape the culture of nonviolence he espoused. Their nonviolent agenda and actions led to the Civil Rights Act of 1964 and the Voting Rights

Act of 1965—concrete examples of big wins. These acts ensured that the same rights that Dr. King fought so hard to establish would be guaranteed for future generations.

In his last major speech, "I See the Promised Land," delivered in April 1968, just one day before his death, he spoke prophetically about the future and the sustainability of the movement. He explained that there would be difficult days ahead, and although he may not live to see it, the people *would* get to the promised land.

Though Dr. King was assassinated by a sniper the next day, his teachings and the nonviolence culture he created (the dream) are still very much alive.

Tenth—*Select, Recruit, and Develop Other Leaders*

A key job of any leader is to find other leaders who can continue the organization and carry on its work. None of these ten points are easy. Doing them all in concert is even more difficult. But it is where leaders need to be spending their time. Those who concentrate on these things will build strong businesses that achieve long-lasting success.

As we have already seen, Dr. King selected and recruited leaders who carried out his philosophy of nonviolence to achieve his goals. Even in the aftermath of his tragic death, the movement held together and pressed forward. His philosophy, vision, and teachings left a legacy that continues to exert a powerful influence throughout the world.

The Southern Christian Leadership Conference has never ceased to advocate the nonviolence approach that Dr. King established as its first president. Subsequent presidents like Ralph D. Abernathy, Rev. Joseph E. Lowery, Martin L. King III, Rev. Fred Shuttlesworth, and its current president, Charles Steele Jr., have sustained the legacy that Dr. King established.

We can summarize the lessons learned from Dr. King's leadership style fairly easily: People who can help organizations achieve their mission are good leaders. People who can help organizations achieve and sustain the mission and culture over prolonged periods of time are extraordinary leaders, even to the point of changing the world.

Takeaway Points

Focus. Leaders concentrate on critical things, not everything.

Continuous improvement. Like everyone else, leaders need to strive to get better. The Leadership Capability Model gives you a road map you can follow to do just that.

Growth is good. The commonality in each step in the model is growth. Talents and capabilities are learned over time.

Extraordinary leaders, like Dr. King, are rare. But becoming as effective as he was should be everyone's goal.

EIGHTEEN

Adversity to Advantage: The Journey Continues

On the morning of July 11, 2008, instead of going to my office at the AT&T Mobility headquarters in Atlanta, I reported to our nearby Perimeter Center retail store. It was 6:30 a.m. when I drove up. At least two hundred customers were already lined up outside the store, and they had been there for hours. We were about to launch the Apple iPhone 3G, and there was great excitement about this new product. The same feeling held sway in our company, because we had been planning the launch for a long time.

At a big retail event, I like to be on the front lines because I can learn a lot by interacting with customers, hearing the questions they ask, and observing how we can improve the buying experience. But compared with the hundreds already there, I was a late arrival.

The Apple iPhone 3G was one of the most anticipated wireless devices in history. It was the high-speed successor to Apple's original iPhone, which hit the market in June 2007 and was named Invention of the Year by *Time* magazine. With iPhone

3G came much faster online speeds, new features like GPS, and the ability to browse while talking. A lot of people were willing to miss sleep to get their hands on one.

As I watched the lengthening line outside the store, I thought back over the path that had brought us here. Like other pivotal points described in this book, our company's journey to this game-changing point had been guided by the principles that undergird the Four Pillars of Success, which I shared in Chapter 2.

Taking the Long View

It started back in 2004 when we made a key decision to simultaneously integrate the Cingular and AT&T Wireless networks and upgrade them with state-of-the-art technology.

We were intent on achieving interoperability (the capability of customers to use the cell sites of each network) as quickly as possible so customers would experience fast coverage and service improvements. "More Bars in More Places" was what our advertising promised. Making the promise reality was my responsibility as COO of Cingular. Our plan was to deliver meaningful service enhancement right away, and then make steady progress toward full integration, which would take two years.

In making these plans, our team recognized an opportunity that was larger than just integration alone. If we were going to integrate more than forty thousand cell sites, why not take it a big step beyond? We could simultaneously deploy 3G—third-generation mobile broadband technology.[1] So when integration was completed, we could roll out a high-speed wireless network that was state of the art in all respects.

In order to achieve the vision of integrating and upgrading at the same time, we had to overcome many obstacles. Never before had two overlapping networks of such size been integrated into one seamless network. So we already were in uncharted waters just doing that. By upgrading, we would be rolling out the first large commercial deployment of HSDPA technology anywhere in the world. We would be planning and executing two huge wireless firsts side by side.[2]

Why was it important to do both? We knew that a new wave of wireless handsets was coming—more exciting and more multifunctional than anything anyone had seen before. Offering iconic, exclusive handsets was a Cingular strategic imperative. At the time of the merger, we already were planning to launch our first such device, the Motorola RAZR. As the name suggests, it was one of the world's sleekest, thinnest phones—the kind of differentiated, signature product that customers value.

Next came the Samsung Blackjack—a "prosumer" product that crossed market segments by combining PDA (personal digital assistant) capabilities for business users with consumer features like video, music, and photos. Like the RAZR, it was a big hit. With 3G adding speed and bandwidth, we would be ready for handsets of the future that would have much faster processors and large storage capacity for music and video. The landscape was changing.

So while there were obstacles to overcome in simultaneously integrating and modernizing the networks, the opportunities made the decision clear-cut to me. Before long, this decision would prove to pay major dividends with the iPhone from Apple.

Convergence

The iPod, introduced in 2001, will go down as a historic breakthrough in personal entertainment. Apple created a product that was all about *my music*, anywhere, anytime. Since the mid-1980s, wireless had been advancing a similar breakthrough in personal communication—first with voice, then with text, and ultimately with any form of media: *my communications*, anytime, anywhere.

Looking back, it was inevitable that that these forces would come together at some point.

One such point happened in 2005 with a device called the ROKR. It was developed by Motorola with Apple's involvement to integrate iTunes technology that would allow the ROKR to hold about one hundred songs. Cingular was the exclusive wireless carrier for the ROKR.

To this day, I think some of the coolest commercials our company ever produced were our ROKR spots. Aimed at the youth market, the product was successful even though it did not become a real blockbuster. It did reveal larger possibilities—both about phones of the future and the rising expectations of customers.

The ROKR led to a solid relationship between Apple and

Cingular. When Apple began work on a wireless phone of its own design, they already knew a lot about us—including our commitment to leadership in broadband and our deployment of 3G that was then underway.

I was one of the first people to see a working prototype of the iPhone. It was an exciting product. The design and functionality were very different from anything previously seen in wireless— very clean, intuitive, and Apple-like. There was not a doubt in my mind that this device was going to be a game-changer.

Now it was my responsibility to communicate the potential to our CEO, Stan Sigman; our board chair, Randall Stephenson; and the rest of the board. I knew this would be a landmark product, and my enthusiasm was convincing to them as well.

At the same time, we would be using a different business model than we had had before. Traditionally, wireless companies buy handsets from the manufacturer at full price and subsidize the consumer's purchase as an incentive. The agreement with Apple was a revenue-sharing model. In many ways, this was as revolutionary as the device. Yet our leadership stepped forward to seize the day.

Reflecting on all of this following the launch of the iPhone 3G, it was clear to me that the principles on which the four pillars are based had made the difference all throughout the process.

- *Plan for success.* We planned and built our high-speed network to support products that did not yet exist because we knew there was exciting potential ahead.

- *Take risks.* At every stage of the story there was risk in any course we took. The risk of being overly cautious always was the biggest, in my view.

- *Recognize opportunities.* Transformational technology was on the way in handsets. We were not sure exactly what it would look like, but our job was to be ready at the right moment.

- *Overcome obstacles.* There were many obstacles, from engineering challenges to selling others on the possibilities for success. Some of the biggest obstacles involved multitasking our way through simultaneous integration and modernization. Thanks to the tremendous effort of our network engineering team, we went from having two separate and disconnected networks to having the fastest, most advanced wireless network in America. We accomplished every objective we had set out to achieve.

By the time we closed the store on July 11, every iPhone 3G in stock had been sold. The same thing was repeated at every AT&T retail location throughout the country. Not a single one was left anywhere.

I went home that night convinced I had seen a turning point in the public's embrace of high-speed wireless as a ubiquitous part of life.

For many years, leaders throughout the wireless industry had been making bold predictions about what would be possible one day through our products and services. That day came on July 11, 2008—and there is no going back.

"One Day"—Every Day

A basic theme I have tried to deliver throughout this book is that for an aspiring leader, each day holds the promise of turning opportunities into significant stepping-stones. There is no such thing as an ordinary day when nothing happens—unless we choose to overlook or avoid that day's inherent possibilities.

Because of the nature of my journey, I have had an unusual number and range of life experiences that drive home the lessons I've related here. My hope is that my story can make these ideas intensely real for readers who have not gone through a revolution as a child and learned to adapt to a new life . . . or been on the front lines of massive technological change . . . or (as yet) had opportunities to lead a team in overcoming dramatic challenges like hurricanes and market turmoil.

The truth is that once these concepts become vivid, they never leave you. Every new day dawns rich with moments that used to seem inconsequential but now are meaningful strides in learning, growing, and becoming more effective.

Looking Ahead

The month of July seems to be my time for changes. From July 2008 when the iPhone 3G was introduced, my thoughts go back to July 1962, when this remarkable journey of mine began in earnest.

The factors that made my success possible started, first and foremost, with an incredible act of courage by my parents, who sacrificed it all to give our family the opportunity to pursue a better future and to turn our adversity into my advantage.

I was able to turn that future they imagined for me into reality as a result of the education I received and the opportunities I was afforded by our free enterprise system, a system based on entrepreneurship that truly makes the United States the land of opportunity.

I believe the American dream is still alive and that education and entrepreneurship together are its key enablers. Through the years I have observed the power of this combination when the two forces work in tandem. Together they lead to personal success, business success, and societal success.

In every nation on the planet, there are young people who will have remarkable futures ahead of them—*if* this combination of education and entrepreneurial possibility becomes an integral part of their being. This is why I work with kids through JA Worldwide. JA programs teach the key concepts of work readiness, entrepreneurship, and financial literacy—concepts that can change lives, businesses, and societies.

So now my work continues with JA, the Boy Scouts, and, of course, AT&T—creating experiences to convince the youth of the world that life can be more than they ever dreamed if they get an education and use it to bring their own best ideas to reality.

I want this ongoing journey to be their own plane to freedom, helping to lift them above their limitations and landing them where their opportunities have no limits. I want the same for *you*. So . . .

Journey on! Obstacles welcome!

Acknowledgments

My life's journey has been an incredible adventure, and I am deeply grateful to the many people who have helped me along the way. I first want to acknowledge my parents, Rafael and Andrea de la Vega, who sacrificed everything to provide a better future for my sister, Barbara, and me.

I am also deeply grateful to Ada and Arnaldo Baez (my second set of parents), who raised me in the U.S. from the age of ten until fourteen and treated me as their own son. They taught me what it takes to successfully start your life over again (from scratch).

Maria, my wife, has been a terrific partner for more than thirty-two years. I would not have had a successful journey without her love, support, and understanding. She has always been at my side and provided the encouragement needed to overcome the many obstacles we have faced together.

I have also been fortunate to have the love and support of a great extended family. My *abuela* (grandmother) Julia Diaz

Gomez taught me the value of a good education, and my Aunt July Pelaez gave me her unselfish love.

Throughout my career I have been lucky to work with many outstanding people. Roger Puerto hired me out of college. I remember telling him at the time that all I wanted was a chance to prove myself. And I got that chance. Thank you, Roger.

Dale Register gave me my first big break by recruiting me to work at Bellcore TEC in Chicago. Dale is a great change agent, a terrific executive, and a good friend. The weather in Chicago was cold, but the people were warm. As a result, we had a great quality of life there.

During my journey I have also been privileged to work with many excellent executives who served as role models. Working directly with Duane Ackerman, Dick Snelling, Rod Odom, Don Strohmeyer, and Judy North at BellSouth, and with Lynn Lindquist at Bellcore TEC made a huge impact in my life and career. Judy gave me my first big opportunity to run a sales organization, which became a turning point in my career. Lynn at Bellcore TEC took a risk and placed a young Hispanic executive in a critical role in his operation. They all taught me how to run a great business with the highest integrity. At Cingular, I was fortunate to have the opportunity to work with Stan Sigman, one of the best and most respected executives in the wireless industry. Stan taught me how to "grow the business" and with a "let's get 'er done" attitude. He also taught me all I know about rodeo!

At the new AT&T I have had the privilege to work with a very talented team led by Randall Stephenson, our chairman and CEO. Randall is a great leader and a great person. I am thankful for all the opportunities he has given me and for the great direction he is providing for the nation's number one telecommunications company.

There are many friends I want to acknowledge for the encouragement they provided me in the writing of this book. I especially want to thank Maria Schnabel, former head of Hispanic public relations at Cingular Wireless, who continuously encouraged me to "tell the story" and inspire young people. Miguel (Mike) and Alicia L. Suarez also provided constant support and were some of the first people who persuaded me to write the book.

There are far too many colleagues to thank over a career that spans more than thirty years. But I want to acknowledge the teams that helped me successfully deal with the pivotal points in my journey. The teams at Bellcore TEC, BellSouth Broadband & Internet Services, BellSouth Latin America, Cingular Wireless, and at AT&T Mobility have a special place in my heart for the sacrifices they made to help us successfully navigate the turbulent times we faced together.

I also want to acknowledge the great contributions of three people who helped to make this book a reality. Paul B. Brown helped me put the manuscript together and provided many helpful suggestions on how to best communicate my extraordinary journey. Sam Pinkus helped me negotiate the contract while he faced a difficult personal situation. And Lea Agnew was terrific in helping me bring the stories about Cuba to life.

I will be forever grateful to Andrew Young, former U.S. ambassador to the United Nations and Atlanta mayor, for the time we spent together discussing the civil rights movement and

Martin Luther King's leadership style. I will always remember the insights of this incredibly humble man who played a key role in the movement that transformed America.

Finally, I want to acknowledge the American people, who welcomed a young Cuban boy at the age of ten, without his family, and without a penny in his pocket, to its shores. I am living proof that the American dream is still very much alive and that the U.S. is the greatest country on the planet. It is difficult to express in words the deep gratitude I have for this great country of ours for opening its doors, the doors of opportunity, to me and my family.

—RALPH DE LA VEGA

Career Timeline for Ralph de la Vega

I've been blessed with many interesting jobs in my life. It can be confusing to try and keep track of them all, so I designed this career timeline to help the reader correlate key positions in my

Ralph de la Vega - Career Timeline 1974-1994

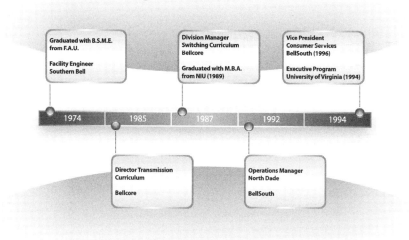

Graduated with B.S.M.E. from F.A.U.

Facility Engineer Southern Bell

Division Manager Switching Curriculum Bellcore

Graduated with M.B.A. from NIU (1989)

Vice President Consumer Services BellSouth (1996)

Executive Program University of Virginia (1994)

1974   1985   1987   1992   1994

Director Transmission Curriculum

Bellcore

Operations Manager North Dade

BellSouth

career with my various Pivotal Points. Given all that has happened to me, and the number of opportunities I have had, I have broken down my career timeline into two phases. The first phase covers the first twenty years of my career, and the second phase covers what has happened since. The book covers the entire career timeline but focuses on the last dozen years (1997–2009).

Phase 1

1974—Facility Engineer, Southern Bell. Graduated with a bachelor of science in mechanical engineering (BSME) degree from Florida Atlantic University. I was hired right out of school by Southern Bell and placed in the Initial Management Development Program (IMDP) as a facility engineer in Plantation, Florida. The IMDP program was designed to develop high-potential college hires (proving my grandmother was right when she insisted that I continue on to college).

1985–1990—Director/Division Manager, Bellcore TEC. In 1985 I accepted a rotational assignment at the Bell Communications Research (Bellcore) Technical Education Center in Lisle, Illinois. At first I was responsible for the development of the transmission curriculum and the transmission laboratories at the center. Following this assignment I was promoted to be responsible for the switching curriculum and switching laboratories. During this time I was responsible for the development of the new multi-vendor switching labs. And while all this was going on, I earned my MBA from Northern Illinois University to help eliminate a "yes-but" (Yeah, Ralph is a good manager, but he doesn't have an advanced business degree) that might keep me from advancing further in the organization.

1992—Operations Manager, BellSouth. Responsible for network operations in North Dade County, Florida for BellSouth. The responsibilities included the engineering, installation, repair, and construction of the telecommunications network. This was one of the divisions that was impacted by Hurricane Andrew in 1992.

1994–1996—Vice President Consumer Services, BellSouth. Responsible for sales, service, repair, and collections of consumer services for the state of Florida for BellSouth. During this time, I completed the Darden Executive Program at the University of Virginia (1994). My time at Darden proved to be a great learning adventure and helped to further improve my educational background.

Phase 2

The next phase of my career has been filled with unique assignments that included starting a new business (broadband services), running wireless operations in eleven foreign countries (Latin America), integrating two companies as a result of the largest cash merger in U.S. history, and running AT&T Mobility, the wireless unit of AT&T. The career timeline for this phase is shown at the top of the next page.

1997—Vice President of Network Operations, BellSouth. In this position I was responsible for all network operations in the states of Florida, Alabama, Louisiana, and Mississippi. My job was to deliver more than $4 billion in revenues while leading more than fifteen thousand people.

Ralph de la Vega - Career Timeline 1997-2007

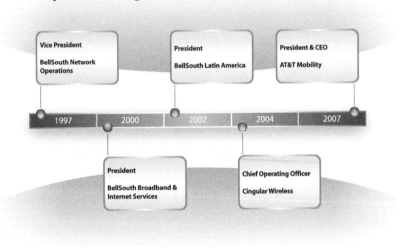

2000—President of Broadband & Internet Service, BellSouth. In this position I was responsible for rolling out broadband services throughout BellSouth's territory. It was basically like running a startup company. I was charged with the task of leading a cross-functional team responsible for all aspects of the new technology. We started with thirty thousand customers at the end of 1999 and grew the business to more than six hundred thousand customers by the end of 2001, making us the fastest-growing broadband provider in the United States.

2002—President, BellSouth Latin America. In this capacity I was responsible for the wireless operations serving more than eleven million customers in eleven countries in Latin America (Argentina, Brazil, Chile, Colombia, Ecuador, Guatemala, Nicaragua, Panama, Peru, Venezuela, and Uruguay).

2004—Chief Operating Officer, Cingular Wireless. As the COO for Cingular wireless, I was responsible for sales, marketing, network operations, technology planning, and customer service. I was also responsible for the integration of Cingular Wireless and AT&T Wireless.

2007—President & Chief Executive Officer, AT&T Mobility. In this capacity I am responsible for the nationwide operations of AT&T Mobility, wireless unit of AT&T. AT&T Mobility generates over $49 billion in revenues (on an annual basis) with over 77 million customers and more than seventy thousand employees. In October 2008, I also assumed responsibility for AT&T's consumer markets.

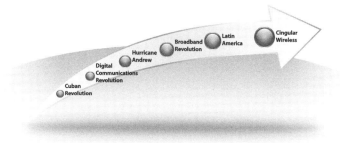

Notes

Chapter 4

1. Adapted from the Lewinian experiential learning model, named for Kurt Lewin, described by David A. Kolb in *Experiential Learning* (Upper Saddle River, NJ: Prentice Hall, 1983), 21.

Chapter 5

1. In late 2005, SBC (the majority partner in Cingular) acquired AT&T and renamed the combined company AT&T. Cingular became wholly owned by the new AT&T in December 2006 as a result of the new AT&T's acquisition of BellSouth, which had been partners with SBC in owning Cingular. After the merger, Cingular was renamed AT&T in early 2007.

Chapter 7

1. From Kolb, *Experiential Learning,* 4.

Chapter 16

1. John M. Bridgeland, John J. DiIulio Jr., and Karen Burke Morison, *The Silent Epidemic: Perspectives of High School Dropouts* (Washington, DC: Civic Enterprises, 2006), 5, http://www. civicenterprises.net/pdfs/thesilentepidemic3-06.pdf.

Chapter 17

1. Donald T. Phillips, *Martin Luther King, Jr. on Leadership*, (New York: Warner Business Books, 1998), 55.

2. Martin Luther King Jr. *Stride Toward Freedom* (San Francisco: Harper & Row, 1958), 101.

3. Ibid, 71.

4. Andrew Young, *An Easy Burden*, Baylor University Press 2008, 200.

5. Ibid, 203.

6. Ibid, 202.

7. Phillips, *Martin Luther King, Jr. on Leadership*, 162.

8. Ibid, 163.

9. Ibid, 157.

10. Young, *An Easy Burden*, 224.

11. Phillips, *Martin Luther King Jr.*, 205.

12. Ibid.

Chapter 18

1. 3G allows wireless downloading and surfing at high speeds with simultaneous voice and data capability.

2. The AT&T Mobility network uses HSDPA/UMTS technology (High Speed Downlink Packet Access/Universal Mobile Telecommunications System).